INSIDE

A memoir by
Otto Bryan

As told to
Diane Russell

Dedication

This book is lovingly dedicated to Otto's Lord and Savior, Jesus, and the faithful family of God who mentored and loved this broken man.

"For he hath looked down from the height of his sanctuary; from heaven did the LORD behold the earth; to hear the groaning of the prisoner; to loose those that are appointed to death." (KJV)

~§~

.

Acknowledgements

It is impossible to write a book without a lot of assistance and encouragement. Throughout his life, Otto Bryan had friends who told him he should write his story. He resisted, saying he was no one special. I suggested he illustrate it and he agreed to at least try.

We were both in our seventies when we started, Otto writing and illustrating while I pushed, prodded and edited. He'd finished his childhood chapters when due to age and illness, he couldn't continue. So I took on the job of finishing it.

Over our thirty-five years of marriage, we'd exchanged many letters. I had kept all his letters to me, filed year by year, and used those letters to complete his story. The first draft was huge when I finished it, so my sister, Dorothy, offered her excellent writing and editing skills to help. The two writing groups I belong to, South Lyon Writers Group and First Writes, gave me valuable feedback. My friends, Bara, Bev, Ron and Linda proofread and friends at my church, Family Life Community Church encouraged me. I could never have finished without all these wonderful people and am truly grateful for them.

Diane Russell

Otto's Story

Too many children still grow up in family situations like I did, with an immature Mom who turned her back on the abuse her husbands piled onto both of us. She didn't have a happy or good life herself, but in the end, love won out for both Mom and me. For Mom, it was that she finally found a kind and faithful husband. For me, it was good friends who cared, the love of a woman, the family I'd always wanted, and my best friend, Jesus.

When I started writing my story, it was very difficult to look back on my childhood and what I was as a young man. It meant re-living my nightmares and especially things I did—and am still very ashamed of—as an immature adult. My hope is that by reading my story, you become aware that too many children grow up like I did. These children are so damaged in one way or another that many die young, are in prison or mental institutions as adults. I was one of the few lucky ones to live out a full and productive life.

~§~

Yours, in Christ,

Childhood

Today I sit in a Michigan state prison with a life sentence. As I look back, I ask myself how my present circumstance happened and why I wasted my life. I grew up bitter, hating most everyone, and was on a fast track to nowhere before I committed the crime that placed me here.

Many of the things that happened in my life seem like dreams now. There were some good periods, even a few happy times, but far more were bad. I try to forget the bad or to ignore them as if they never really happened. That's not always successful. I can try, but my experiences growing up shaped who I now am.

Oregon, 1937

I was born Robert Otto Bryan in Salem, Oregon in 1937

Mom

to Myrell Leona Bryan and her husband, Earrol Wallace Bryan. Mom's mother, Sadie, told me my father was an abusive man and died when I was a baby, but I learned as an adult that she'd lied. My father lived with his birth family in Minnesota and died when I was about ten. Sadie also said he had a terrible temper. Was I destined to be like him when I grew up?

When I was sentenced to life in prison in 1974, Mom told the police that my father had been no good, she couldn't take any more of his getting drunk and beating her, so when I was ten months old, she left him. Mom married again when I was very young, but that didn't last long either and I don't remember him. I think in all

1

she married seven times.

For most of my early childhood I lived with my grandparents (Sadie and Walt) in Idaho, bouncing back and forth between them and Mom as she headed in or out of another marriage. I heard Mom tell my grandmother that she never wanted me. Mom had a talent for dating and marrying drunken, abusive men, who also abused me. The last time I saw her was in 1959.

I wanted to love my mother; children are supposed to. But how could I love her, when she dragged me into her cruel relationships and never came to my aid when my stepdads mistreated me? I didn't like it when I was out playing with my friends and she'd call me home. Instead of "Bobby," she pronounced it, "Baby." She did this even after I told her it embarrassed me.

Even when it was just two of us, Mom ignored me and never hugged me. The only time she and I were physically close was when she'd clean the wax out of my ears with her bobby pin, with me laying my head on her lap. I craved more times like that. *What was wrong with me, that she didn't want me or love me?*

South Dakota

The first stepdad I remember is Dale. We were moving again—it seems we made a hundred such moves during my childhood—and had everything we owned tied on an old flatbed truck. I don't remember where we were going this time, perhaps South Dakota. I was about seven and had a little dog named 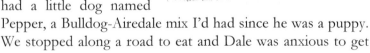 Pepper, a Bulldog-Airedale mix I'd had since he was a puppy. We stopped along a road to eat and Dale was anxious to get going again. Pepper didn't come back when we called, so Dale ordered me to get into the truck, and we pulled back onto the road. As we drove off, I looked back and saw Pepper running down the road after us. "Stop! Please stop!" I cried. Dale just kept driving. He refused to stop, even though I was crying. Finally, grudgingly, at Mom's pleading, Dale stopped so we could get Pepper.

We eventually settled in Wagner, a small town in South Dakota. We lived in an old gas station about a quarter mile out of town. The gas pumps were gone and the big garage front door was boarded over. Wagner was small, and was a gathering place for American Indians in that part of the country. In the summer, they came from every direction and held a huge celebration with dances, pony races, circle gatherings and bonfires in the evenings. The summer gathering wound up with a big parade down the main street of Wagner, with Indians wearing their feathers and trappings. For a kid, it was exciting, especially because many of them set up their tents and camped just across the highway from our gas station home. One of the Indians invited me to the camp and told me how he made his headpiece. "I'd love to make one!" I told him, so he showed me how.

While we lived in Wagner, I was in the second grade. Mom's brother, my Uncle Lyle, returned from the war. He arrived at our place in his brand new white Packard. In it, he told me, was a big box, just for me! However, since the next day was Friday (a school day) he made me wait until the weekend to open it.

We spent the weekend, Uncle Lyle and me, and had fun. He showed me how to make a toy parachute with string, a handkerchief and a machine nut. Before he left, Lyle also made me a nice slingshot. However, I couldn't wait to open that big wooden crate!

When I finally got to see what it was, I was the happiest, luckiest kid ever, jumping and squealing and laughing! My uncle had brought me the neatest electric train set there ever was. He spent the weekend helping me set up the whole track system all around the garage floor. We made tunnels, curves and bridges. He told me he had the train set shipped clear from Germany, which made it even more special to me. I wished I had a Dad to show me how to make things like the Indian and Uncle Lyle did.

After Uncle Lyle left, I came home from school to find my train set gone. Dale had sold it and I was devastated. Dale slapped me, said "Stop your crying. You sound like a big baby." That was the last time the train was ever mentioned. I tried to stay out of Dale's way as much as I could; he always told me I was a bad boy, a lot of trouble.

Dale grew even more foul and abusive to both Mom and me, angry most of the time. Many nights I lay in bed, scared, listening to Dale's drunken cussing and yelling. I heard him slap Mom over and over. In the mornings, she'd try to hide her swollen or bruised lip from me. I did my best to be very quiet. I spent most of my childhood being quiet, avoiding attention and staying out of the way. Why did Mom marry men like him? Was her father like that when she was a child?

Cleveland

From Wagner we moved to a tiny three-room house in the outskirts of Cleveland, if you could call it a house. It was a tar-paper shack with an outhouse. Our water came from a well with a hand pump that left a scar

4

over my left eyebrow. Each morning it was my job to pump a pail of water. I had to prime the pump by pouring in water, then pump the handle like crazy. One cold morning ice had formed on the handle. As I pushed down, my hand slipped. The handle slammed me over my eye. I bled like a stuck hog and had a black eye for days.

An old turned-over rowboat in the yard was my hideout, and I went there when Dale was drunk and yelling at Mom. He didn't care which one of us he hit, and if I tried to protect Mom, he'd hit both of us even harder. Mom had a job at a dry cleaner as a press operator; I don't remember what kind of work Dale did, but he went to work or somewhere some of the time.

I was born with a problem; I sometimes wet the bed. A doctor said I had weak kidneys and bladder and said I would outgrow it. When I was young and lived with Mom's folks, I also walked in my sleep. Grandmother Sadie took me by the hand, walked me around a bit and then led me back to bed. In the morning, I wouldn't remember it. When we lived with Dale in Cleveland, I'd sometimes dream I was standing at the toilet, only to find in the morning I'd either wet the bed or peed on the floor in the closet. Dale insisted "You're just too lazy to get up and go to the bathroom!" Whippings were his way to solve my problem.

We moved into the city of Cleveland and rented the upstairs of a large house. Mom and Dale played cards on Friday nights with the couple who lived on the ground floor. Mom made sure I was asleep before going downstairs. One night, I walked in my sleep. There were two windows in my corner bedroom; one opened over the front porch roof and lawn, and the other  opened on the street side, with a straight drop to the sidewalk. Directly below that side street window was a basement window, set below the sidewalk in a hole. So that people wouldn't fall into the hole, it was surrounded by iron spikes.

In my sleep, I opened one of the my bedroom windows, crawled out onto the porch roof, slid to the edge and off– onto the cold, wet grass below. That woke me up! I sat, bleeding from scratches down my chest and belly, trying to figure out just how and why I was there. I went to the door that led directly upstairs and found it locked. I went around the house and through the big front window, I saw everyone sitting at a table. I knocked on the window. Mom's eyes grew large as she quickly jumped up.

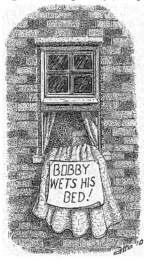

Had I decided in my sleep to open the side street window, I would have been speared on those iron spikes. I didn't get any sympathy, even though I could have been killed. To top it off, when Dale found out I'd also wet the bed, I got another beating. Someone nailed that street-side window shut, briefly.

It was only briefly, because Dale came up with an idea he thought would stop my bed wetting. He hung my wet sheets out that window with a sign "Bobby wets his bed!" for all my third-grade friends to see.

When we moved to a single-family house in Cleveland, Mom went to work in a factory. I don't think Dale worked, as he was always around the house. I hated being home with him when Mom wasn't there. He bossed and berated me and did some things to me that I never told anyone about, not even Mom.

When Mom was at work, Dale would force me to masturbate him in some way–first with my hands, later my mouth or anus. It hurt and was disgusting to me, but if I refused, he'd hit me on the chest with his fist (where no

6

bruises showed). Then he'd threaten to hurt me worse if I told Mom or anyone else. 'I will put a smile on your face that you'll always regret, if you do!' he'd say.

I felt terribly dirty, ashamed that I might have done something really bad for this to happen to me. Dale told me often enough that I was a bad boy, so I must have been. I didn't dare tell Mom, because she might be beaten even worse than me. I didn't think she'd actually do anything about it anyway, because she never did when she saw him hit me.

I did accidentally hurt Dale once and paid for it–later it seemed like a minor victory. We lived in a basement apartment then, with a living room, one bedroom, a kitchen and a bath. I slept on the living room couch. In the bedroom, over my parents' bed, was Dale's precious mandolin. He was always very strict and serious about it; had a rule that no one but him touch it and that went double for me.

I had few toys, so when home alone, I found it great fun to use Mom and Dale's bed as a trampoline. I was bouncing up and down and as I bounced up I saw Dale's precious mandolin going down! It landed just before I did, and in the same spot. I'll always remember that big crunch. I frantically tried to think of a reason to explain what happened, but couldn't. I was dead… just knew it… and expected it.

Of course, I received a heck of a beating. I had huge red welts all over my back, butt and legs (as always, where no one at school would see them). My mother said nothing, as usual, but she did doctor my wounds afterwards. She was probably as afraid of Dale's anger as I was, so I could never count on her to take my side.

Oregon

We moved again, this time to Goshen, Oregon. Mom

7

got a job working at a bar and dance hall. As usual, her absence meant more physical abuse from Dale, but at least he'd stopped forcing me to do the sexual stuff to him. When Mom was there, he'd still hit and yell at her. He disliked her working as a barmaid. He accused her of being involved with other men, but she always denied it.

I'd just started the fourth grade when we moved again from Goshen to Oakridge, thirty-five miles away. Dale acquired some property on a hill. The road up the hill was a steep dirt road. When it rained (as it often did in Oregon) we could not drive up the hill. We'd have to park the truck at the base of the hill and walk up. Even on dry days, I was afraid our old truck wouldn't make it or would slip off the road and tumble down the hillside. I always suspected that the move to Oakridge was to get Mom away from her barmaid job. Certainly, that hill kept us away from everyone.

On that hill, we lived in a World War II army tent with everything we owned crammed inside. The tent had no windows, just two doors. It had wooden side walls with a canvas roof and an outhouse in back. Mom made makeshift rooms inside with piled belongings and boxes dividing the spaces into sort-of rooms. I slept on an army cot in one corner. To get to the school bus in the mornings, I had to make my way to the bottom of the hill. Getting home meant I must climb back up again.

I loved one thing about living on that hill. In spring and fall, it was in the path of migrating ducks and geese. At night, lying on my cot, I could hear the birds flying over our hill. To me, it sounded like they flew so low I could reach up and touch them, if only I could see them in the dark. I wished I could fly away to somewhere else like the geese did.

Another thing I liked about living on that hill is that I was never alone with Dale. Even though he still bossed and abused me, my mother was always there too. She still didn't stick up for me or try to ease the situation, but just her presence kept Dale from more sexual abuse.

Then one day, Mom surprised me by telling me she planned to move off the hill and into the town of Oakridge. I didn't know if that meant we were leaving Dale behind or not, and I didn't ask. I hoped we'd leave him, and I expected Mom to tell me I would go and live with my grandparents, Sadie and Walt. Every time Mom's marriages went bad, I'd be left somewhere until Mom married again and came to get me.

Detroit

Mom said no more about leaving the hill and moving into Oakridge. But one day when we were alone, she gave me some good news about my grandparents. This time, however, it wasn't Mom's parents, but rather my father's parents, Otto and Nellie Bryan. I'd been told that my middle name, Otto, came from this granddad, but I'd never met him.

I was one very happy boy when Mom told me I was going to fly on an airplane to meet my grandparents in Detroit, Michigan. Grandpa Otto paid for my plane ticket. Not only was I delighted to get away from Dale, I got to fly and meet some new family members.

I was thrilled to climb aboard a big plane. A stewardess watched out for me during the flight. As we bent to look out the window, she pointed out interesting things on the ground below. She also made sure I had snacks. When we had a three-hour layover in Chicago, she took me to the apartment she shared with another stewardess. They fed me and treated me wonderfully before returning me to the airport to board

9

the next plane. When I landed in Detroit, another stewardess took me to where my grandparents waited for me.

Grandpa Otto and I hit it off from our first meeting. Otto was a portly, kindly-looking man whom I immediately trusted. He was an Electrolux vacuum cleaner salesman. He also worked part-time as a night watchman at Detroit's tall Penobscot building. Sometimes Grandpa took me to his night watchman's job on weekends. I loved that! I'd make the rounds with him to punch the clocks, and in between rounds I'd spend the time on the rooftop, looking through the telescope mounted there. I could look all over the city or up at the night stars.

Grandma Nellie was a tall, slender somewhat-reserved woman who worked as a receptionist at Grace Hospital in Detroit. She wore her waist-length hair in a big bun on the back of her head. When she hugged me, it felt like she had a suit of armor under her clothes. She always wore her girdle. I never understood why, because she was not fat.

Grandma Nellie and I played a sort-of game. When she wanted me to do something, she didn't tell me. Instead, she'd hint all around at what she wanted, and I would act like I didn't understand. She'd say "Bobby, the porch needs sweeping," and I'd nod but didn't go and do it. When Otto would come home, Nellie told him about it. Otto would wink at me, and say "I know…" so then off I'd go sweep the porch. Otto always played along with our game, and advised Nellie to be more direct and simply ask me to do what she wanted. I loved Nellie, and enjoyed our little game.

Both Otto and Nellie showed me a totally different way of life from any I'd known. They had a nice two-story house on Petosky Street, and we went to the nearby Catholic church. For the first time, I had nice clothes to wear, even a suit and tie for church and special events. We went to restaurants, museums and Sunday afternoon drives over the bridge to Canada. We saw *The Nutcracker* and some other plays. They paid for my YMCA summer camp and swimming lessons. I started the sixth grade in a big Detroit school.

I wanted to learn to play a musical instrument, so Grandpa Otto took me to the YMCA on band night to see what instrument I might like. When we got home, Grandpa asked me if I'd decided and I said "Clarinet!"

Days later a man showed up at our apartment with a brand new clarinet. Otto arranged for me to have private lessons. In a short time I was playing first chair in the grade school band. I practiced hard and often; before long I was able to play a solo for family day at school. I played *The Clarinet Polka*, one of Grandpa's favorites.

My days in Detroit were so different than the life I'd lived before, I wasn't sure if it was all real. Did people really care about kids like Grandpa Otto and Nellie cared about me?

A friend of mine, Allen, attended a Catholic boys' military school in Monroe, Michigan. I liked his school uniform, so when I said I wanted to attend the same school, Grandpa and Grandma enrolled me. I learned later that it cost them several hundred dollars to send me there–a lot of money in those days.

I was fourteen and midway through my first year at the school when I was awakened at midnight by Sister Luellan, one of my favorite nuns. She told me my mother was there. As soon as Sister Luellan turned away, my mother took hold of my arm and out the door we went. I never asked her where we were going; she had always up and moved me before, without ever telling me. Mom put me in the car and told me to stay in the back and on the floor. A man I didn't know was in the car too. Later I learned he was Mom's real birth father, not Walt, the grandfather I knew. Walt was Mom's stepfather.

Mom snatched me away because Grandpa Otto had refused to send me back to my mother, accusing her of ruining my life with her marriages, divorces and constant

11

moving. That was the reason she resorted to kidnapping me. I'd never told Grandpa about my stepfather's abuse. I truly missed my Grandpa and needed the love and stability that he and Nellie gave me. And yes, Mother had married again, this time an engineer for the Southern Pacific Railroad, Jimmy Neil.

These constant moves may also be the reason I did well when locked up. Prison gave me stability and a sense of routine that I'd never had as a child. It must seem strange to anyone who grew up in a real family that someone could find stability in a prison. I learned that if I obeyed the rules, stayed occupied, minded my own business and picked my friends carefully, I could manage okay. No one in prison beat me, either. Until I had a real family, prison wasn't hard on me. Later, the hardest thing was being separated from those I loved.

Oakridge, Oregon

Mom, her father and I sped out of town and drove all the way to Oakridge, Oregon. I learned that while I was in Michigan, Dale had killed my little dog Pepper. I loved that mutt, and it broke my heart.

Oregon is a beautiful state, and I had both good and bad memories of Oakridge. The town was quiet and small, with the Willamette River rushing alongside. The railroad yard was there to assist trains up the steep River Pass. At Oakridge, they hooked up powerful booster engines needed for the climb.

Sometimes other boys and I would hop on the train at the edge of town and ride it to the summit. Then we'd hitchhike back down the highway. Once, a school friend and I managed to toss bikes on a flatbed car. While riding our bikes back down the steep winding highway, we never had to pedal once. What a ride that was!

Mom didn't care where I was or what I did, so I spent hours tramping around the countryside and in the mountains. There were many things for a boy to do there–run in the woods, climb hills and trees and enjoy the clear cold rivers and creeks.

I camped and fished along the Willamette River, quite often alone because my friends had real families. During the week I went to school, but after class on Friday I'd stay away from home until Sunday evening, spending many hours climbing the trails in the hills.

I loved the Willamette River and spent a great deal of time near its small fork. I'd fish or hunt squirrels or spend time at the big marsh between our lot and the river. Sometimes, I did nothing but lie still and watch the birds dart from cattail to cattail.

Mom and I had moved continually, so I never spent one whole year in the same school until I was a freshman in high school at Oakridge High. As a result, my schooling was constantly in a state of flux and I didn't have friends for long. Growing up always on the move placed me in different schools and communities, but I learned how to quickly 'read' those around me and that served me well over the years.

We lived about three miles from school and I could have taken the school bus. However, I hated riding it because the other kids had better and nicer clothes. Day in and day out, I wore the same khaki pants and shirts. A girl made a comment about my clothes and from then on instead of riding the bus, I ran to school. I was used to running so many hours in the hills that I felt I could run all day. I'd watch the others get on the bus, and then I'd tear out and be at the school before the bus arrived. As soon as the last class let out, I'd take off for home the same way.

I joined the school band and was soon promoted to first chair in the clarinet section. I spent as much time as possible during breaks and lunchtime to practice in the band room. I also practiced at home in my little room. I loved to mimic the records of Benny Goodman and Artie Shaw. It was strange, but I loved playing the clarinet for an audience; it gave me confidence. Yet, in a classroom if a teacher called on me, my mouth went dry and my tongue wedged itself to the inside of my mouth. I could only mumble, even when I knew the answer. I never raised my hand to volunteer any information. Mom usually ignored me and my stepfathers told me to shut up so often that I mostly talked just to other kids.

My music always smoothed things out for me. A music group of four men who worked at the lumber mills during the week played at Saturday evening dances and asked me to join their band. They encouraged me to play solos and gave me an equal share of the money, even though I was just a kid. I even got a chance to dance with some pretty girls from Oakridge High.

One day at school, I told a friend about all the running I did. After school, I cut across the field where the track team was practicing and my friend saw me. The coach asked "Can you run the quarter mile?" and I proved I could. I wound up easily beating the school's best runner. That year I won every 440 event clear up to the state championships in Eugene. But that was my finish. Before the race, I was so nervous and afraid to fail that I heaved my stomach out.

There were lumber mills everywhere in Oregon. My best friend, Dean Halstead, and I liked going to the local mills on Sundays when they were shut down for the weekend. We'd jump around on the big logs floating in the ponds. Or we'd climb the high narrow elevators that carried the sawdust and scrap wood to the top of the incinerators for burning.

Dean and I also spent a great deal of time in the woods, climbing, camping, swimming or fishing. We were nearly always together. If I happened to be at his house at meal time

14

(and I quite often arranged to be there) his parents always welcomed me. Some weekends Dean's dad would drive us to an old logging road and leave us to camp. Dean and I gathered ferns all weekend. We'd fill up a trailer then Dean's dad would drive us to Eugene, where we'd sell the ferns to a florist.

I spent as little time at home with Mom and Jimmy as possible. I wish I had a dollar for every time I raided someone's garden for things to eat rather than face Jimmy at mealtimes. At Dean's house they always made me feel welcome and treated me like a son.

When Dean couldn't be with me, I spent a lot of time at the river. At one point the river moves fast around a bend, and the rapid current creates a backwash and a small sandy beach and pool. This pool was great for fishing or swimming.

Dean and I decided we'd build a tree house in the trees that grew at the edge of the backwash. Dean's dad gave us the

wood, spikes, nails and ladders. We found an old window and chimney pipe in a house that had burnt down. I "borrowed" the tarpaper we used to cover our tree house from materials my stepdad Jimmy had. I figured he was always too drunk to ever finish the house he'd started.

By the time we finished our tree house, we had a stove, table, fruit crate shelves, a double bunk and even a porch/deck. We build a stone fire pit on our little beach and cooked trout over the fire. I loved it there and slept more nights in the tree house than I did at home. To the others it was a nifty place to come, but to me it was more of a home than the one I had.

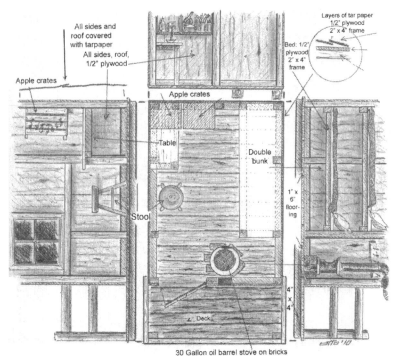

An accurate drawing of the Oakridge, Oregon tree house on the Willamette River

Labels in drawing:
- Layers of tar paper 1/2" plywood 2" x 4" frame
- All sides and roof covered with tarpaper
- All sides, roof, 1/2" plywood
- Bed: 1/2" plywood 2" x 4" frame
- Apple crates
- Apple crates
- Table
- Double bunk
- 1" x 6" flooring
- Stool
- 4" x 4"
- Deck
- 30 Gallon oil barrel stove on bricks

Jimmy Neil

Jimmy and Mom lived in a trailer about three miles outside of Oakridge, where he had begun to build a small house. On the back of what was to be the attached garage, he had built a small storeroom. This was my bedroom. I had a cot, a kerosene heater, and a rod to hang clothes on. There was no electricity, inner walls or insulation.

Jimmy was a stocky, nasty-tempered, whiskey-drinking, man. A boxing champion in his Navy fleet, when he got drunk he used Mom as his punching bag. He made it pretty clear he wasn't pleased about my presence. He never missed a

16

chance to belittle or cut me down. He especially liked telling me that I was worthless and he named me Stupid.

When we sat down to eat, Jimmy said, "Remember, you're eating *my* food–food I worked very hard for and I put on our table!" That's why I practically lived at the tree house. Instead of eating Jimmy's food, I caught and cooked fish, stole from gardens or ate at friends' homes. If I couldn't eat at home, I'd have to find food any way I could. Mom and my stepdads never taught me that it was wrong to steal.

Near the end of the school year, Oakridge School held our ninth grade dance in the gym. Dean's dad said we could drive his car. The day before the school dance, Jimmy shocked me by telling me he would let me take his car if I'd promise to be very careful with it. I told him I already had plans to go with Dean in his dad's car. Jimmy insisted we use his. I should have known that his offer could only bring trouble.

The night of the dance, Dean and I drove Jimmy's car. Knowing how fussy Jimmy was about the car and knowing he'd kill me if I brought the car home scratched, we were as careful as we could be. At the school, we parked as far as we could from other cars. That evening we spent as much time baby-sitting that blame car as we did inside with our friends.

When I arrived home I heard Jimmy yelling and cussing, clearly drunk again. He was standing in front of Mom with a butcher knife in his hand, yelling at her, "Take it from me, I dare you! Just try!"

As I stepped through the door, he hit me in the face, knocking me down the steps. I fell out the door, scraping my back on the rough edge of a cement block.

I lay there for a couple of minutes, waiting for the pain to let up. Jimmy slammed the door shut. I heard him say something about my "hot-rodding" his car. I couldn't believe it! We'd treated that car like a baby.

I made it to my little room and sat there for a long time. I couldn't see in the dark, but I could feel my shirt was soaked and sticking to my back. I could hear Jimmy yelling at Mom in his drunken state across the lot, but I couldn't hear what he was saying.

The yard light came on and the trailer door slammed. I heard Jimmy in the driveway between the trailer and the unfinished house. He came busting into my room, still cussing, and said "Tell me the truth! You raced my car, didn't you!" I didn't answer, too scared to say a word.

He slapped me, and I curled up into a ball on the cot. He pounded his fist into my bleeding back, calling me stupid again. He left, slamming the door. I never shed a tear until I heard the trailer door slam shut. Then I sat there, crying and shaking.

I couldn't hear any more yelling. Worried about Mom, I crept outside the trailer and listened. All I heard was Mom crying. I was more afraid for Mom than for myself.

Maybe our nearest neighbors would help. Their house was dark, but I pounded on their door until they came. I was crying, frantic and begged "Please call the sheriff! My stepdad is beating my mother!" The lady saw the blood on my back and wanted to clean it, but I wouldn't let her. They would not call the sheriff for me because they didn't want to get involved. Why do grown-ups always stick together against kids?

I had to do something! I remembered that Mom's 22-rifle was stored in my room so I could use it for squirrel-hunting. I didn't have any shells, so I ran to the neighbors again. "Can you give me some .22 shells?" The husband just told me to go home and to bed. Back in my room again, I fell asleep crying. When I awoke before daybreak, I decided I was going to leave home and wanted to get away before Jimmy woke.

I couldn't go into the trailer to get any food, but Mom had stored jars of pickled cucumbers, blackberry jam and canned stew that Grandma Sadie had given us in the tool shed. I helped myself to those. I sneaked out the back of the lot and down to the river, put everything in the tree house, then headed to Dean's house.

Dean's mother saw me, didn't asked questions but cleaned and dressed my torn back with loving, tender care. She fixed us breakfast and told me, "You need something else to wear; here's a shirt that Dean has outgrown." I loved Mrs. Halstead. Why couldn't Mom be more like her? I'd always wanted Mom to love me, but maybe she didn't know how to love that way.

For the next three or four months I stayed in the tree house at night and often ate at Dean's house. Neither my mother nor Jimmy ever came looking for me.

I did get even with Jimmy, though it was a terrible thing I did. I was with some friends in town, at the trucker café that was a popular hangout. A block behind the café was the parking lot for the rail yard. Jimmy's white Dodge was parked there, and I knew Jimmy had been called in to work. When all of us kids later split up, I couldn't resist giving his Dodge a visit. Jimmy always parked as far away as possible from the cinders, water and mud.

I opened the car doors all the way, and turned that white Dodge into a black one. Inside and out, I smeared black cinder gunk over every inch. As a parting shot, I took my pocket knife out and cut the valve stems on both rear tires, knowing Jimmy only had one spare. I walked away, turning to say "I did this for the abuse and beatings Mom and I took from you!" I was sure Jimmy would think of me when he saw his car, but he never came looking for me.

My First Time in Trouble

I was so used to just hanging out and doing whatever I felt like doing that when the time came, I didn't register for tenth grade that fall. I watched the others getting on or off

19

the bus each day, but living as I was, I figured school was out of the question. I had no way of keeping my clothes clean without hanging around home. I rarely went home to see Mom, but if I did, she didn't seem to care what I was doing. Of course, Jimmy never did care–he didn't want me around from the start. I didn't even see Dean and his parents now that Dean was back in school.

I got to the point where I didn't want to even see my mother, and certainly not Jimmy, especially after what I'd done to his Dodge. I hadn't seen him around at all since that evening but did notice that, instead of the car, there was a pickup in his driveway. When I saw Mom, neither of us brought up the subject of Jimmy's car. She didn't ask if I'd trashed his car and didn't say anything about my not being in school, either.

I really didn't know what I was going to do. I was just a young, very angry kid. It was pretty obvious that I couldn't live in the tree house forever. Not long after that, my immediate future was determined for me.

I became friends with a boy named Dinky. His uncle owned a bar along the highway, across from the café the kids hung out at. The back porch of this bar stuck out over a river bank above the Willamette River. It was braced in the back by large poles. Dinky's uncle paid him to clean the bar on Sunday afternoons. I went with him a couple of times, and his uncle trusted him enough that he let Dinky do the job alone. Dinky didn't need a key, because he could climb onto the back porch and get inside from there.

These bar-cleaning sessions were a bonanza for me, because I got to eat while there. Dinky was allowed to heat and eat a couple of the ready-made sandwiches, along with a pop or two. During our last cleaning day, we decided we'd take some beer and sandwiches to my tree house. Surely, his uncle would never miss those four beers and sandwiches. How wrong we were!

The next day, walking in town, Sheriff Duffy stopped me and drove me to his office. The jail was a one-cell affair, connected to the back of Duffy's office. He told me he knew all about my activities at the bar the night before, and that Dinky had told him everything. He said Dinky's uncle was charging me with theft, for stealing the beer and sandwiches. Duffy said if my parents would come get me, I could go home until I had a hearing with the judge. Dinky had already gone home. Of course, I didn't want to call Jimmy for his help, and wasn't crazy about calling to ask my mother to come either. Sheriff Duffy already knew where I lived and he called Mom.

I told Sheriff Duffy how Jimmy beat my mother, but it seemed to make no difference. It was a crime for me to swipe a couple sandwiches and beers from Dinky's uncle at his bar, but was it okay for Jimmy to beat my mother. That just didn't seem right to me.

No one came to get me. That evening Duffy fed me, and I spent the night in the one unlocked jail cell. I had clean blankets for a change, was safe and slept well. The next  morning Duffy told me he'd seen my Mom and Jimmy, and that Jimmy refused to come and get me. Since he didn't mention it, I assumed Jimmy didn't accuse me of the car-trashing. I stayed at the jail, and Duffy trusted me enough that he left the cell door unlocked so I was able to clean up, clean his office and eat well.

Neither Mom nor Jimmy showed up for my hearing

before the judge. Without any support from home or parents, the judge said he had no choice but to send me to the Woodburn Reformatory. The next day, Duffy and I stopped at Mom's to get my clarinet, the one Grandpa Otto gave me and that Jimmy had *not* paid for, and we were off.

Wandering

Woodburn, 1952–1953

Sheriff Duffy drove me 150 miles north to Woodburn Reformatory. I saw lots of boys and five large buildings. Three were dorms, another the school and the last, the infirmary. We lived in dorm rooms on the upper floors. The offices, recreation and dining rooms were downstairs. We spent our days in school and working in huge bean fields. When we weren't in classes or working, we were locked in our dorms. We could play ping-pong or pool, watch TV and play other games in the recreation room.

I was a 'hiker chaser' in the bean fields. I sat on a platform on the top of a large pole. As the others picked beans, my job was to watch from my platform and be ready to chase down anyone who tried to escape. Luckily, I never had to catch anyone.

Because I was a hiker chaser, one of the other boys gave me a hard time and we got loud about it. To settle our dispute, we had to put on boxing gloves and duke it out. The kid was bigger than I was and I knew I couldn't whip him. I turned away as if I'd given up and he lowered his hands. Then I spun around and bloodied his nose. After that, we became friends. We both knew I'd gotten in a lucky punch.

One of the counselors in my building liked me and watched out for me. Some weekends he'd take me to visit a family who lived in the town of Woodburn and who even invited me for Christmas. Their daughter, who was three or four years older than I, played the piano while I played my clarinet. How I wished I had a family like that one! The counselor later told me they'd asked about adopting me, but since I still had parents, they couldn't.

In the spring, I was sent to a forest camp on the west coast of Oregon. We lived in small Quonset huts and the larger huts served as a kitchen-and-dining rooms, recreation halls or offices.

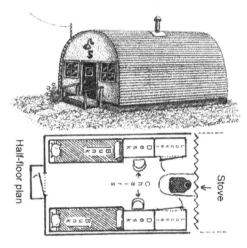

We cleared saplings and brush away from trails, roads, and park areas. We also planted a lot of grasses on beaches to hold down erosion, built benches and log tables for the parks.

One important job we did was to cut down tree snags to prevent forest fires. Snags are old or broken up trees that become dry and powdery. If lightning strikes it, a snag can burst into flames and start a forest fire. I loved this job! It was like camping in the Oakridge woods again.

On one snag-clearing job, the tree was too large for us to bring down with an axe so we used dynamite. I folded over the fuse so the boss could cut if off with his hunting knife. When he did, the blade slipped and buried itself in my bicep, clear to my bone, but I didn't cry. The boss wrapped a belt around my arm to stop the bleeding, lit the fuse and blew the tree down. Then we headed for a hospital. I had that scar for the rest of my life.

One morning a pair of fawns came into the camp. We adopted them, feeding them warm milk from a pop bottle with a rubber glove finger as a nipple. Those fawns had the run of camp. One day they left and that was the last we saw of them.

In camp, I'd had the best time of my life so far. I was surprised one morning to find myself packed up and on my way back south. An officer gave me $25 and put me on a bus back to Oakridge. The driver dropped me off in front of the sheriff's office, and Sheriff Duffy said he'd drive me to Mom and Jimmy's place.

I asked Duffy to let me out at Dean's house instead. Mrs. Halstead was as nice as ever to me. She told me she'd seen my mother a few days ago and Mom had a black eye. That was that! Jimmy was still with her, and I would not live with that cruel bully. I wanted to say goodbye to Mom before I left. Mrs. Halstead said I could spend the night with them.

Later in the evening Dean and I walked to Mom and Jimmy's. I saw no vehicles in the driveway, so figured Jimmy was at work. Mom greeted me as if I'd only been gone for an hour—not over a year. Mom's eye was still bruised. No smile, no hug, no "good to see you!" All she asked was "Did you run off from Woodburn?"

While we talked, Jimmy pulled into the driveway. Dean left in a hurry, saying he needed to get home. Jimmy was not pleased to see me. He, too, asked me if I'd run off from Woodburn. I could tell he'd been drinking. I expected him to be abusive to me as he'd always been, but instead he started in on Mom, right in front of me. I was furious; that was all I could take.

Jimmy got up to go to the bathroom, and before I left, I decided to give him something to remember me by. At each end of the couch Mom had lamps, one a Japanese warrior, the other a Geisha girl. I angrily grabbed the Geisha lamp,

25

removed the lampshade and stood on the cord, tearing it loose. Mom just stood by, wide-eyed and silent. I picked up the lamp, jumped on the kitchen counter and waited for Jimmy.

As he came through the kitchen, I swung that lamp for all I was worth. Jimmy's forehead split, the blood flew, the lamp shattered as he went down. He was out cold, and I was at the door before he hit the floor. Mom said, "You'd better get out of here!" She didn't need to tell me. As I left, I said, "Mom, tell Jimmy that was for all the black eyes and abuse he'd given you and me."

There was a chance Jimmy would report what I did to the police. I couldn't go to the Halsteads' and get them involved. The only thing I could do was leave town.

Leaving Home, 1953

I was sixteen years old and completely on my own. I'd pretty much raised myself anyway, was nearly grown, had never been part of a family or had a home like my friends did. I walked to the rail yard in town, figuring I'd hop the train to Klamath Falls. I spent the rest of the night sleeping in an old caboose behind the roundhouse.

I could have tried to get back to Detroit to my grandparents. I'm sure Otto would have sent me bus fare. However, I felt ashamed for having left the military school without telling them. Once I'd left and because all I concentrated on was surviving, I never wrote or talked to any of my grandparents again.

Early in the morning, I saw the railroad workers' parking lot. Because Jimmy was a railroad engineer, I checked the train schedules. I wanted to make sure he wasn't going to be the engineer to Klamath Falls. Before I picked a train to hop, I also made sure Jimmy's pickup wasn't in the parking lot.

I'd hopped trains a number of times before and knew where and when the train picked up speed. As I waited to hop onto a train again, I thought of my first time I hopped.

Dean and I had met a couple of cute girls who invited us to a Lowell High School dance. We didn't have any way to get to Lowell, so got the bright idea of hopping on a train. The only train moving in the right direction that evening was pulling nothing but oil tanker cars. Tankers have only a narrow platform with a steel railing, which is not much to hang onto. We didn't want to miss the dance, so jumped on and held on as tightly as we could.

The tankers were empty, meaning the train went faster than usual. We passed Lowell at what seemed like a hundred miles an hour. There was no way we could jump off without killing ourselves. When the train finally slowed down near the Eugene rail yard, we jumped off. What a sight! Our greased hair stood up by itself, and our faces, skin and clothes were black with soot. My nice new white cords were two-toned: black in front, off-white in back. We never got to see those cute Lowell girls again.

Now, I was ready again to hop on a train, alone this time, and about to run for my life.

I hopped on a train and reached the Klamath Falls rail yard late in the day. I figured as long as I was near a rail yard that I'd find lunches to eat. I hadn't eaten for a couple days and was hungry. I knew railroad workers kept their lunches in lockers, so decided to steal a few lunches to take with me. My plan didn't go smoothly. I found the bunkhouse, but two men were inside. When one left, I grabbed a lunch pail and ran. The other man came out yelling but I outran him and hid under a loading dock. I opened the lunch pail. Nothing but an empty thermos bottle, sandwich wrappers, and an apple core! I should have learned then that crime didn't pay, but no one had ever taught me that. After all, my first theft in Dinky's uncle's bar taught me that swiping sandwiches and

27

beer gave me one of the best years of my life at the forest camp.

I had no way of knowing where any particular train was going and didn't want to go back toward Oakridge. As I walked, I saw a vegetable patch at the back of some properties along the tracks, helped myself, and filled up on tomatoes, radishes and carrots.

I walked until I saw a train coming. It was already picking up speed so I ran beside it and jumped to grab on. Just as I reached for the ladder step, my foot caught one of the railroad ties. Down I went into the cinders. I sat there watching as the caboose sped by, then brushed the cinders and dirt off my face. Scared and shaking, I thought "If there's a God, he must have kept me from falling under the train wheels!" This was my first real brush with death. I found another train to hop, and then every train yard or depot with bunkhouses kept me fed.

In Denver, tired of hopping trains, I stole a motorcycle that I'd spotted through an open garage door. I rested and watched the garage from across the road in a small park until dark. I was in luck; no one came home to turn on the lights. I entered the garage, spotted a couple of sleeping bags on a workbench and a ball of heavy twine on the countertop. How convenient! I tied one of the sleeping bags to the 'cycle and kicked the motor on. The 750 Triumph worked just fine and I wouldn't have to keep hopping trains. I thought I was so clever.

On the outskirts of town, I pulled into a small shopping center parking lot to re-tie the sleeping bag to the bike. Done with that, I spied a woman putting her shopping bags into her car. She slipped her purse from her shoulder and dropped it onto the front seat of the car, then took the empty shopping cart back to the store. Her car was unlocked. I was hungry, but did I dare? Before she got back, I'd taken the money from her purse, left her billfold behind and took off down the road. I didn't get a lot of money, but enough for some food

28

and gas.

I had to ditch the 'cycle when the motor quit, so I hopped trains until I got to Las Vegas.

Las Vegas, 1953

Even though I hadn't seen either of them in years, I knew my mother's brothers, Darrel and Lyle Luke, lived in Las Vegas. I remembered that Lyle gave me that train set after the war, but hadn't seen him since. I arrived in Vegas with filthy clothes and no money. I needed to urinate, but I was too young and filthy to go inside a nearby casino. The gas station bathroom was locked. I spied a dumpster in an alley and used it for privacy. Just then, a police car drove by and stopped. I was afraid to tell him who I was or where I was from, so he took me to the police station where I was charged with lewd conduct. While the policeman called the juvenile authorities and no one was looking, I took off.

I found Lyle and Darrel's phone number in a telephone book, in their big-as-day Luke Brothers Construction ad and tore it out. I had no money to make a call so wandered around, checking every public telephone in hopes of finding some forgotten coins.

At the bus station, a lady saw me checking the row of public telephones and she offered me money to call after I told her I was trying to reach my uncles. I showed her the ad with the phone number and company address and she drove me there on her way home.

My uncles were not glad to see me, so I felt uncomfortable with them and their families. Uncle Lyle let me sleep in a small camping trailer next to his garage. I met their children, my four cousins, for the first time and my aunts fed me. The Luke Brothers did finish carpentry in Vegas, so I asked my uncles for a job but they said I was too young. One evening, Lyle said he'd just heard from my mother. She'd moved to Des Moines, Iowa, and was getting another divorce.

29

Lyle suggested I enlist in the Army. Because I was not yet seventeen, I needed my mother to sign for me. My uncles bought me a bus ticket and called Mom to tell her I'd be on my way. She said she'd meet me at the Des Moines bus station.

Aunt Alta took me shopping for badly-needed new  clothes, then I waited in her car while she took care of business inside another building. I watched cab drivers pull into a cab company lot nearby. On their way to their own cars, the drivers dropped small white drawstring bags through the taxicab door mail slot. "Are those money bags?" I wondered.

Aunt Alta checked the bus schedules; I could leave tomorrow afternoon and arrive in Des Moines the next day.

That evening back at my uncle's house, I kept thinking about those mail slot money bags. The next morning it was still on my mind, and I thought of a way I could "fish" those little bags out through the cab company door slot. In Uncle Lyle's garage I found his fishing box, cut off a length of fishing line and tied a small hook to one end. I rolled it up in a piece of cardboard and shoved it in my pocket. I was ready.

The next morning, both my aunts took me out to eat and then to the bus depot. They hugged me and left. As I waited for my bus, again I thought about that cab business. It was not far; I could see it down the street from the bus depot.

I had my bus ticket, but when my bus came, I didn't get on. I decided instead I'd go to the cab company that night. I could catch the bus the next day. I spent the afternoon and evening sightseeing and cat-napping in the bus depot. About two in the morning I walked down the street, got out my fishing line and made my way to the cab company door.

I began playing the line and hook around; it was just like fishing in the Willamette River! Successful, I'd hooked something and pulled out a bag. I didn't bother to look inside, but shoved the bag in my pocket and dropped the hook back into the slot again. Once more, playing the hook and line, I snagged another bag. I rolled up the fishing line and left.

Back at the bus depot, I went into the men's bathroom. I opened a bag to find a fat roll of money. I emptied both bags and crammed the money into my pockets. I thought the police might be looking for me so I spent the next seven hours mostly hiding in the depot bathroom.

Once I was on the bus, I felt safer. I slipped into an empty seat in the back and as the bus pulled out of the depot, I promptly fell asleep. I woke when we later stopped for food. Everyone else left the bus to eat, but I stayed behind, pulled the money out and began to count it. In my hands I held $722–more money than I'd ever seen before! I stuck the hundreds- and fifty-dollar bills inside one of my socks, the twenties and tens in my other sock, and the singles in my right front pocket. Then I went into the depot to get something to eat.

I thought I was pretty clever and grown up, getting all this money. In truth, I was a very insecure child who never developed a normal conscience, because I'd been raised by cruel and immature adults who didn't know right from wrong themselves. Mom was still like a child, searching for someone to take care of her.

Mom was not at the bus depot in Des Moines, but I had arrived a day later than planned. I didn't have Mom's address or phone number to let her know I was finally there. All I could do was wait and hope she'd come back. In the middle of the afternoon, I heard my name over the loudspeaker. Mom was at the depot desk.

We went to the motel where she lived and talked until late. I told her I wanted to enlist in the Army and needed her to sign for me and she said she would. She didn't tell me if Jimmy took out his anger on her after I smashed him, but

31

said he never reported me to the authorities. Mom also told me she'd spent most of her money on a used car, and needed to find a job soon. I slept in an easy chair in her room that night. The next day we went to the Army recruiting office and she signed my enlistment form.

Before she left me there, I surprised Mom. "Here's some money for gas, and I'd like to pay for a restaurant dinner." After we ate, I gave her a little package wrapped in napkins from the restaurant and said "Don't unwrap this until you get back to your motel." I gave her half the robbery money; I was proud to finally be a man taking care of her!

I was sent to Camp Chaffee in Arkansas for basic training. I loved it. Because I'd worked in the Woodburn forestry camp, I was in great physical shape and got through it just fine. An officer gave us a pitch about paratroopers. It sounded exciting, and besides, I liked the uniform with the bloused pant cuffs and jump boots. "Sharp!" I thought, "Just for me."

We had jump training in Fort Bragg, North Carolina. Even though I was in good shape, our training was grueling. We ran–never walked–anywhere, did push-ups and practiced jumping off five- or six-foot high platforms.

After Fort Bragg, I was sent to Fort Campbell, Kentucky. There a warrant officer suggested I join the division band. I moved into a barracks with band members and honor guards. Our main duty was to march in parades around the country.

Fort Campbell is only an hours' drive from Nashville, so a fellow band member, Lance, and I spent a lot of free time there, driving in Lance's new Oldsmobile convertible. I dated a Nashville girl named Nina and Lance dated Nina's best friend. The girls wanted to see us jump, so we left Lance's car with them and hitch-hiked back to the base. The jump field had bleachers for spectators to watch the three or four hundred guys floating down all at once. How would the girls identify Lance and me? We decided to stuff a roll of toilet paper between our chests and reserve chutes. As soon as we left the plane, we let our rolls of toilet paper unwind. It worked just fine … the girls got to see us coming down.

The girls weren't the only ones who saw us. We barely hit the field when Lance and I were chewed out. We were barred from leave for thirty days and spent two weeks waxing and buffing floors. The girls were happy; they got to see us jump and had Lance's car to use for the month.

Washington, 1954-1956

Army life wasn't the fun I'd expected, so I made another in a long string of bad decisions. I left the base and hitch-hiked to Nashville to spend time with Nina. I ran out of money, and couldn't find work there. I still had my Army uniform, and a fellow in uniform could easily hitch a ride, so off I went.

I got to the Nashville airport and was lucky; there was a military cargo plane about to leave for Nellis Air Force Base near Las Vegas. Once I left the plane at Nellis, I could hitch a ride to Las Vegas.

I called my uncles and learned that my mother now lived in Vegas too. She was married again of course, this time to a man named Earl Moreland. My aunt picked me up and took me to the trailer park where Mom and Earl lived.

Earl was a large tanned man with a worker's rough hands and a strong and steady handshake. He worked for a landscaping company in Vegas, but had been a farmer most of his life. He didn't have the bossy, arrogant attitude that Mom's other husbands had, and he didn't drink. After I visited them for three or four days, I was ready to move on. Mom was finally in the good hands of someone who treated her right.

I had to decide where I wanted to go and how to get there. The military would be looking for me, and maybe the Vegas police. Hitchhiking might make me more of a target, but did I have the nerve to steal a car? I wouldn't know

33

unless I tried. I walked around the parked cars behind the casinos and found a Buick with the keys in it. Hooked to the visor was a string of gas credit cards. *What a break for a car thief!* I congratulated myself and pulled out of the parking lot. Once out of the city, I decided the best thing for me to do was to turn myself in as AWOL.

The closest military base I knew of was Fort Lewis in the state of Washington. On the way I drove through Oakridge, Oregon. The only changes I noticed were a few more houses. The school, café and truck stop were still the same. The bar where Dinky and I stole the sandwiches and beer was still there too.

I didn't know if Jimmy still lived in the same place, but someone had finished the house and cleaned up the yard. I wondered if the old tree house still existed. I didn't stop to see it, nor stop to see if the Halsteads still lived in the same place.

When I crossed into Washington, a state police car pulled up behind me. I was pretty sure he was checking the car license plate. He put on his lights and siren; I knew I was caught.

He took me to the jail in Kelso, Washington. I pled guilty to car theft and was sentenced to one-to-fifteen years in the Monroe Correctional Complex. I was discharged after a year and a half. The Army gave me a dishonorable discharge at the same time.

Midwest and Vegas Again, 1957-1960

After my release I traveled around the Midwest for a couple of years, most of the time in stolen cars or motorcycles. Stealing motorcycles was less trouble than cars and used less gas. I'd cruise down alleys until I found a car easy to get at and I'd siphon the gas for the 'cycle. Sometimes, I'd hop on a train for a free ride.

I usually slept in a sleeping bag outdoors. In bad weather, I asked farmers if I could spend the night in their barn or shed. They were always willing to help, never asked questions and often gave me something to eat. God bless those farmers! I found trucks parked at a trucking company also a good place to sleep. Several times, a driver woke me up before he took his truck to a job. A time or two, someone gave me a couple of dollars.

I tried finding work at landscaping companies, but there were no jobs. Back in Vegas, I asked my uncles for work, but they turned me down again. I finally quit trying and looked for ways I could get enough money to keep going. I thought of the homes surrounding the Vegas Desert Inn Golf Course. Those were expensive homes! Many of them had sliding-glass doors on the back, overlooking the golf course. Easy to get into, and I told myself that these people had more money than they needed.

I attached a small rubber ball to the handle of a glass cutter. With this tool, it was simple to cut a circle near the handle of a sliding glass door and punch the glass circle with the rubber ball. The glass would pop out, and I could reach my fingers inside to dislodge the lock and open the door. The first time I entered one of the golf course homes I found a display case in the hall. Inside, labeled and lying on some felt, were some odd old coins. I knew I couldn't take these, because I had no idea how to get cash for them.

The evening was not a total loss, however, because I found a two-gallon fish bowl, filled–not with water–but with bills and silver dollars. "A bonanza!" I thought. The next day, I saw a headline in the *Las Vegas Sun* "Burglars Overlook $50,000 Coin Collection."

In 1959, I met a man named Dan who didn't work but had plenty of money. I discovered his source when I joined Dan and together we burglarized several homes. Our partnership didn't last long. When Dan was arrested, he named me as his accomplice. We were each sentenced to prison in Carson City, Nevada. In prison, I hated my life, hated myself and had nothing to live for. I tried to kill myself by cutting my wrists. I didn't die; and swore I would never again join up with someone else to commit a crime. If it were something I couldn't do by myself, I would not do it. I couldn't trust anyone, so was better off alone.

While I was at the prison in Carson City, Nevada, I started corresponding with a girl named Marlene, who lived in Omaha, Nebraska. Marlene's brother promised me a landscaping job. When I was released, I took a bus to Omaha. The boss at the landscaping company was a terrific man, willing to help his workers in any way he could. When I bought a Ford Crown Victoria, he co-signed for the loan. That Ford was cream color on top and gray on the bottom. I cleaned and waxed it every week.

As proud as I was of that car, it was a shame what I eventually did with it. I'd fallen for a girl named Sandra. I loved her and her folks and hoped to become part of their family. Then, out of the blue, Sandra dropped me for another fellow. I was so deeply hurt that I quit my job and drove back to Vegas. Once again, my uncles refused me a job. I left and headed north. I felt worthless and the more I dwelt on my situation, the more depressed I became. I had nothing but the car I still owed money on, no job, no family, no friends. No one cared if I lived or died, so I didn't care either.

I'd just passed through Beatty, Nevada, when I stepped on the gas. Soon I was going over 90 mph. I whipped the wheel to the right and the Crown Victoria roared off the road into the desert, bounding over sagebrush and sandy mounds and moguls, one after another. I bounced around from one side to another inside the car. Finally the car rolled over twice and stopped. It was ruined, but surprisingly, I was still alive!

I climbed out and found I had a few minor bruises but no serious injuries. For some reason, I'd been saved from death for the second time. I walked back to the highway, leaving my Crown Victoria behind. I owed my former boss money for that car and felt guilty that I couldn't repay him when he'd been good to me.

No one cared about me, so I began caring less and less about anyone else. I decided to never risk getting close and being dropped again. It was a lonely life, and at times I wanted to kill myself just because no one cared if I lived or died.

I spent several months hitchhiking around the southwest, stealing a car when I could. When I had a car, I slept in it. Otherwise, I slept outside, in empty trucks or wherever I could. If I could find a temporary job, I'd work hard. I was pretty good at drawing and sometimes sat sketching in a bar where someone might buy my drawing. If I couldn't find work, I'd steal to stay alive. *Why did I even try to live?* I wanted love and a family, but wouldn't allow anyone to get close enough to me for fear I'd be hurt and rejected again. I was falling apart mentally, just wanting to die. I had no idea where Mom was so I decided, one more time, I'd go see my uncles to say goodbye.

Missouri, 1961-1972

I went to Bethany, Missouri, after one of my uncles told me that Mom and Earl lived there. Before I ever saw them again, I was arrested for a burglary and sentenced to one to fifteen years. I spent two years in the Missouri State Penitentiary. When the lieutenant governor commuted my sentence, I moved on to St. Louis.

Soon after I got to St. Louis, I was drinking, got into a fight and was arrested for assault. The police sent me to a mental health center to determine my mental condition. My IQ scale score was 124 and they found–in the words of the report–"no signs of any organic brain damage." The report also said I blamed others for my own failures. The probation officer recommended a minimum sentence based on my traumatic childhood, and I spent two years in the Jefferson City prison, west of St. Louis.

I always adjusted well in prison, perhaps because I could depend on someone to feed and give me a place to sleep, something Mom, my stepdads or uncles never did. I got into weight lifting, working out, so I wouldn't be messed with by other inmates.

The parole supervisor at Jefferson City contacted a Mrs. Lois Danker, to see if she might help me. Lois was a social worker and the head of an organization (Metropolitan Service Association or MSA) that helped with home and job placements after a man or woman was released from prison. Lois wrote to introduce herself and I was surprised anyone would take an interest in me and decide to give me a chance. If someone had cared when I was a kid, my life might have been worthwhile, but by then I thought I was a complete failure. I hated myself for messing up my life, hated my Mom and her abusive husbands so I expected that if Lois got to know me, she wouldn't care about me either.

I also thought she was trying to convert me to Christianity, but it was too late. As a kid with Grandpa Otto, we went to his Catholic church, and I believed in God but I'd lost all that faith. When Lois suggested I work with an MSA volunteer, I agreed until I found out he was a "Reverend." I was angry and told Lois, "I don't think God is going to fill my cup with success. I have to work hard myself to make it in life! My nature can't be changed now." But Lois didn't give up on me.

Because of her backing, I was released early from the Jefferson City prison in 1964 and went to live with Lois and her family. I was very nervous about staying with the Dankers, but the whole family welcomed me. Lois' husband, Professor Frederick Danker, was a Lutheran pastor, an instructor at Concordia College and author of scholarly books. As brilliant and educated as Frederick was, he also was very down-to-earth. We sometimes shared a beer, and introduced me to Greek coffee, which he served in tiny cups. The coffee was very dark and thick as tar but I enjoyed being with, and drinking coffee with, Frederick.

I'd always remember one day at the Dankers'. Lois had

spent a couple days at the prison to visit other men and women she worked with. When she returned home, she told us about an inmate who was a very good artist. Lois brought out several pieces the inmate had done and praised his work. I thought how much better I was at drawing. I'd done the quick sketches in bars and other customers would pay for them. I didn't say anything, but the thought stayed in my mind.

I found temporary jobs in St. Louis, but was still a troublemaker. I stayed with the Dankers for a while, but after a few months, moved out and didn't tell the parole officer or the Dankers where I lived. I owed money to the Dankers, who had helped me buy a car. I was picked up for stealing; however the police didn't have enough proof, so dropped the charges.

I got involved with another parolee, Ruby, whom I was not supposed to see, and still spent some weekends with the Dankers. I did all right until Frederick accepted a sabbatical assignment in Europe. After they left St. Louis, I got in trouble with the law again.

I met a woman in a St. Louis bar. She seemed to like me and I spent all the money I had on her, picturing a romantic night ahead. Once my money was gone, she was no longer friendly. She taunted me and I grabbed her. She yelled and someone called the police. She told the police I was trying to rape her. It wasn't true, yet I didn't stand up for myself or fight the charges. As a kid, I'd learned that defending myself with authorities never did me any good. I was sentenced to six years in the Jefferson City prison.

In prison, I starting drawing and found the confidence to begin to paint. When the Dankers returned from the sabbatical in Europe, Lois came to visit me at the prison. I did so well with painting that she put some of my paintings on display in shows and sold some for me in a gallery. I did two paintings that were pure fun fantasy and a large one of Jesus sitting at a small table with his hand extended to people who looked on. I called it *The Invitation*. As I worked on it, I wrote this in a letter to Lois:

```
Been working on my Invitation all
evening. Having a heck of a time with it
too, so just gave it up for the night. So
far this evening he's had three different
right arms. Looking in a mirror, I'd paint
the arm in, take it out, put it in, take it
out! Afraid I started something that's just
too much for me. Hate to admit it but
that's the way it's turning out.
```

I didn't even know what Jesus had looked like, but knew he watched out for me when I caught my foot trying to catch a train and when I rolled my car in the desert.

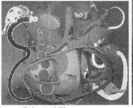

Troupe 807   *Celestial Fantasy*   *Invitation*   *The Robe*

Again, because of Lois, I was released early. The Dankers set up a showing of my artwork at a Methodist church and *The Invitation* was in the center hallway. I went to my exhibit and saw, gathered around my painting, a dozen little kids. They moved back and forth, standing up tall and squatting down and talking … then I realized they were looking at the eyes of Jesus in the painting, which seemed to follow them around. One little girl reached up and touched the extended hand of Jesus. I'd never forget that. I gave the Dankers that painting and another of my paintings for Christmas, which I called *The Robe*.

In prison, I had met two brothers, Bob and George, and we kept in touch after we were released. I stayed in the Dankers' home again. Lois found me a job at a small plastics company, Marex, that made home décor products. I loved working there. It was a "start at the bottom" job, but I was grateful for it. I learned to make molds and designed some new products for Marex. I made duplicates of artwork for the local art museum's gift shop as well. The boss noticed my dedication, promoted me to supervisor of the night shift. After that, I was promoted to assistant plant superintendent.

I was staying at the Dankers' home and first met Kay in 1968 when my prison friend, George, introduced us. The Dankers spent the following summer in California (where Frederick was teaching) and I stayed in their St. Louis home to help Lois' elderly mother. The day before the Dankers returned, I moved out and married Kay.

Kay had a daughter from her first marriage. We bought a new home in a nice area and enjoyed furnishing and decorating it. I didn't contact the Dankers because Kay and my step-daughter were my family, instead of them.

Married and working for Marex, for the first time in my life I felt pride in who I was and what I was doing. In addition to my job at Marex, in the evenings I designed and made my own home décor products to sell in area gift shops. Kay didn't work and I tried to convince her to handle my décor business by taking samples to stores and collecting money for those that sold. Instead, I had to do it myself; Kay had no interest in helping me and spent most of her afternoons watching TV soaps.

I was successful, yet at times, I'd suddenly feel so sad and lonely that I'd go down to our basement or into the garage to hide so Kay couldn't see how I felt. I couldn't tell her that I actually did not know how to live! I felt that I did not fit in anywhere, certainly not with a family.

Things suddenly fell apart at Marex. The sales representative forged thousands of dollars' worth of orders. Marex geared up to fulfill the orders, hired more workers, and worked hard to make and stock them, then discovered the orders were fake. By then, Marex was deeply in debt and we cut to a skeleton crew, working at half wages. It was finally impossible to keep going and save the company.

I was thirty six years old when Kay and I lost all the things we owed money on, our house and new furniture, one by one. I found other jobs, but because of my greatly-reduced wages, creditors were on the phone or at the door all the time. Every new job I got, I soon lost because bill collectors repeatedly contacted me at work. Our marriage became sour as well and Kay talked about leaving me. Was I being dropped again? Losing my family–something I'd always wanted–was too much!

Besides a day job (for as long as I could keep one), I took a job working at night, driving a courtesy bus for a hotel in St. Louis. I was home just long enough to clean up and leave again for the hotel. The bill collectors couldn't catch me to repossess my car. When I was at work at the hotel, I hid it in the back of their parking lot.

As if things weren't bad enough, I almost lost Kay, but not through divorce. She had uterine cancer and the surgery came close to killing her. The cancer was gone, but the medical bills were not. We did not have the $7,000 to pay them. I began to worry and lose control of my thoughts. I found myself developing fixations, like being locked on the number four. Why "four" I had no idea, but I told no one about it.

We were again at the breaking point of our marriage, so I moved out. I found a room downtown and drove for the hotel. When I wasn't driving, I was bar-hopping. My fixations steadily got worse. I remembered my friends from the Jefferson City prison, brothers George and Bob. Bob was back in prison again, but George was married and lived in southern Michigan. I called him and he invited me to visit.

A day later I was on my way to Michigan. I found myself counting the telephone poles along the road: one, two, three, four … one, two, three, four … one, two… If I messed up the count by missing a pole, I felt compelled to pull over to the side of the road, back up to where I remembered missing the count and begin counting again.

42

I spent a few weeks with George and Dot in Cassopolis but never told them of my mental problems. Often I almost fell apart and went off alone to pull myself together. When I felt in control, I looked for work. I was job hunting when I did the worst thing I could possibly do.

Cassopolis

The Worst Night

I remember little about the worst night in my life or exactly where I was. Most of what I know is what I heard from the police accounts or what I read later.

It was April 27, 1972, and I was out job-hunting again. I was driving on a gravel road when my car overheated so I stopped to let it cool down. A man saw it parked with the hood up and stopped to assist me. I thanked him and said it would be OK, so he drove on.

I saw a run-down house sitting in an open field of corn stubs that reminded me of some of the shack-like houses Mom and I had lived in. I didn't see a car or anyone around. I knocked; no one answered and the door was unlocked, so I went inside. I was out of money, so maybe I'd find a little here. The place was filthy, pretty much a trash heap, with clothes piled up everywhere and rags strewn throughout the house. The floors were so caked with dirt from the field, it was like walking on the ground outside. Mattresses were piled three to four high in one bedroom. I thought of the Army tent we'd lived in on top of a hill, with everything we owned piled inside and crammed together. However, Mom had kept our tent as clean as she could.

I was about to leave when I heard a car pull up. I panicked, and stepped into the bedroom, where I saw a shotgun hanging on a wall. I took it down, not knowing if it was loaded. The family came in with two very small children who were absolutely filthy, both their bodies and clothes. Those two young children—and another one on the way—had

44

to live in that pigpen! That's when I lost it. My mind went into a fog.

The wife had started a pot of coffee as I stepped from the bedroom into their kitchen. I pointed the gun at the couple and sat down to have coffee with them so I could think. *Caught again; what should I do?* I decided to tie them up so I had time to get away. I tied the man to the bed which was piled high with old mattresses, dirty clothes and blankets. I tied the woman's hands and feet with her pantyhose. Then I picked up the children and placed them in a crib, safe and out of the dirt. That's all I remember doing, but the newspapers said I cut the man's wrists and neck with a knife from the kitchen, then the woman's wrists and neck and left them both to bleed to death.

As I left the house, I stumbled on something on the way back to my car. I got in and drove away. I was shaking badly, so before going back to George and Dot's, I parked the car and just sat for a while, trying to remember what had just happened. I tried to pull myself together. I was still clean; none of that dirt from the house was on me. The next day, I saw the story on the TV news and realized what must have gone on.

I was horrified, scared and shaking. *"Is that me? What did I do? It must be me!"* I hadn't had a nightmare. Why did I do that horrible, terrible thing? I had to get out of there, so shaved off my beard, packed and quickly left, my head foggy. I left for Florida, where Kay and I had once vacationed.

This is an eclipsed report from the newspaper...

The Daily Star, Niles Michigan, Friday, April 28, 1972

CASSOPOLIS A young couple, Tim and Arlene Roderick, and a third child scheduled to be delivered today, were brutally murdered Thursday in their home 2½ miles west of here. Victims were Tim, 23, his 24-year-old wife and her unborn baby. The Cass County medical examiner said the victims were slain at about 8:30 a.m. The knife-slashed bodies were not found until 7

45

p.m. The couple's two children (3 and 1½) were unharmed but hungry.

Apparently they had spent the day in the house with their dead parents, foraging for food. The Undersheriff said the three-year-old was "fairly calm" and able to give officers a description of a man believed involved in the slayings.

The Sheriff called the murders "the most gruesome I have ever seen in my 16 years as a police officer." When he arrived at the house, he was greeted by the two children standing on a couch and looking forlornly out a front window. An officer found the man's body tied to a cot in a small back bedroom with the wrists and necks of both victims slashed.

The woman's body, clad only in a pajama top, was found sprawled on the living room floor in a large pool of blood. The man's legs were bound with shoelaces and nylon stockings to the foot of a steel cot in the smaller of two bedrooms. His body, like that of his wife, lay in a pool of blood. The house was in a state of disarray.

Officers went to every home in the vicinity seeking information about cars or persons seen in the area during the day.

The Daily Star, Niles, Michigan, Saturday April 29, 1972
All leads fizzle in probe of triple murder in Cass

CASSOPOLIS-Investigators probing a triple murder near here admitted they are up against a stone wall and appealed to citizens for help. Numerous leads apparently have fizzled out in the slayings.

The Prosecutor issued a statement: "We have no suspects, and are appealing to the public for information." He asks that anyone who saw any vehicle parked in the driveway or who gave assistance to the driver of a disabled vehicle, call the sheriff's department. The sheriff interviewed neighbors and relatives as possible suspects. However, the questioning proved fruitless.

Autopsies revealed lengths of rawhide shoelaces knotted around the throats of the victims, but deaths resulted from loss of blood, not strangulation. The woman's body was found on the living room floor at their home by a friend who looked through a window when no one answered his knock at the door. The husband's body was lashed to a cot in a back bedroom with slashes on both victim's wrists and necks.

The couple's two children were unharmed but hungry and were taken to the home of relatives. The sheriff's department is in constant contact with the State Police crime laboratory.

The man who stopped to give me help apparently saw the news and talked to the sheriff, who had someone draw a sketch. The newspaper ran the sketches with an update.

Witnesses' sketches; Police arrest photo

My friends, George and Dot, saw the news with my description and an eye-witness' sketches and contacted the police with my photo. I was put on the FBI's most-wanted list. Three weeks later I was arrested in Florida for burglary and the sheriff there contacted the Cassopolis sheriff. Two detectives drove south to bring me back to Michigan. I was interrogated and charged with two counts of first degree murder and one of manslaughter, for the unborn baby.

The sheriff appointed me a public defender, Attorney

47

O'Connor. After the detectives interrogated me for hours, I admitted I'd been in the house and probably killed the couple, but remembered very little. I didn't meet O'Connor until after I'd signed a confession.

I'd seen those poor little children having to live in that filthy place. They deserved something better! O'Connor told the circuit court that he would plea that I wasn't guilty because of insanity.

A doctor prescribed tranquilizers because I was so agitated, and I sat in an isolated cell upstairs in the Cass County jail from May until October. I rarely saw anyone except the jailer on his rounds or a hand through the slot in the door to give me meals. The lights were always on; the only window was down a walkway. It was frosted; if I saw light, I knew it was daytime. I was so depressed I wanted to die, and wished I could see someone who could give me some assistance, anything to clear my tortured mind.

Every day was the same, except when I had an appendicitis attack. A doctor poked around a bit, then left; nothing more. A couple days later, my appendix actually ruptured. I went to the hospital in an ambulance and had it removed. Then, back to my cell again, alone with nothing to do but wait… for what?

In October, I was sent to the Forensic Center in Ann Arbor for an evaluation to determine if I was competent to stand trial because I was still so anxious and confused even with the tranquilizers. Doctors from the Center went to St. Louis to talk to my wife, Kay.

Competency hearing, Judge Michael Dodge, January 11, 1973

The court held my competency hearing and the Forensic Center director, Dr. Robey, said my mental illnesses had increased, even on a large dose of Thorazine, a major tranquilizer used for psychosis. He said that being at the county jail would likely increase my mental illness, and I

48

needed to remain at the Center, under medication, for treatment for several more months before I could be declared competent to stand trial. Because of my bizarre obsession with the number four and other fixations beyond simple depression, he said that I had "chronic, undifferentiated schizophrenia" that was getting worse. He also said that my anxiety was not about what would happen if I were found guilty, but something so frightening that I couldn't pin it down. It was definitely abnormal. My attention span was so short that I still could not remember much about my crime. Dr. Robey said I was unable to assist my attorney in court and so, incompetent to go to trial yet. He questioned if I trusted my attorney, O'Connor, because apparently, I'd been unable to trust most people in my life.

Forensic Center, Ann Arbor

The doctors at the Center had started me on 200ccs of Thorazine, but it had no calming effect on me at all. They kept upping the dose until I was on 1500ccs a day, plus two other medications. I was finally a bit calmer. Other men at the Center were given 200ccs of Thorazine and I'd seen them just sleep for a day or two.

I saw a psychologist for psychotherapy sessions, but don't remember how often. At first, I was so anxious all I felt was panic and bewilderment. I couldn't tell him much of anything. Once I was on the highest doses of medications, I told him about my erratic childhood and my feelings that any time I connected with someone, that person would reject or desert me.

It was nearly impossible to talk honestly with the doctors, because I'd always been afraid of personal conversations, especially with men and even my Grandpa Otto. I never told anyone what Dale did to me because I was so ashamed.

My attorney, O'Connor, had Dr. Emanuel Tanay, a forensic psychiatrist from Ann Arbor, examine and evaluate me for my defense. I saw him twice, once in August 1972 and again in November 1973. Dr. Tanay told the court that my mind was diseased, I had long-term emotional problems and was unable to control my behavior. He said that I could never be set free, that my emotional damage occurred so early in my life it couldn't be corrected. Because I would never recover, rather than prison, he recommended that I be committed to a mental institution.

Twice the Center gave me 'truth serum,' trying to get me to tell what happened with the Rodericks but I still couldn't remember. On so much medication, I was mostly passive and uncaring.

The Dankers knew what I'd done, yet Lois continued to write and encourage me. She and Frederick, with the Center's approval, drove to Michigan to visit me and to confer with the doctors about my therapy.

The doctors knew I liked to draw and paint, so arranged a room in one of the buildings for me to use. I went a few times but couldn't focus my mind on a thought long enough to do much of anything. I had a grounds card because the staff knew I wouldn't try to escape, and spent most of my days just walking around the Center's compound grounds. I was receiving Social Security disability (thanks to Lois', efforts), so had a little spending money. I'd buy malts and hamburgers at the center's cafeteria. By the time I left the center, I'd gained fifty pounds and weighed almost two hundred.

Competency hearing, Judge James Hoff, November 16, 1973

At my hearing, the Forensic Center's Dr. Shapiro, the psychologist I had talked to the most, said he believed I was ready for trial. Dr. Robey said that I understood enough and was able to go to trial as long as I remained on my heavy dosages of medication. He said I was clearly mentally ill, but felt that I could understand my charge and answer questions in a courtroom.

Dr. Emanuel Tanay, the forensic psychiatrist, said at that hearing that my mental condition had become strikingly worse between his two exams. He said that I had a life-long mental illness and had become more withdrawn and uncommunicative, perhaps because of the medication. He still felt that I should be committed to a mental institution for life, rather than be sentenced to prison. My attorney, O'Conner, questioned the fact that I was worse after being at the Center than when I was admitted the first time.

Judge Dodge said because my case was rather complex that it might take three months to bring it to trial. He asked the psychologists if it would be best to return me to the Center rather than the jail and re-evaluate me again shortly before my trial date, rather than put me back into the jail and solitary confinement. The psychologists said it would be best if I returned to the Center.

However, I was sent back to the county jail to wait for trial. I just wanted to die, knowing what I'd done and what might lie ahead for me. After hearing the doctors' testimony, I thought I'd be mentally and emotionally tortured for the rest of my life, no matter where I went.

The Best Night

I sat in an isolated cell upstairs in the county jail again,

waiting to go back to court. I was alone and had nothing to read, no TV or radio. Sergeant Parrish, who was sent to Florida to pick me up and bring me back to Michigan, dropped by my cell to talk for a few minutes. I was still on the heavy medication so sometimes couldn't even talk, but he kept coming.

After several short visits, he asked me

51

if I'd like something to read and offered me a Bible. I was so starved for anything to fill my long hours, I said "Sure!" He gave me a King James Bible, so old and used that the pages were nearly falling out.

When I was a kid in Detroit with Otto and Nellie, they tried to teach me about God. I loved going to midnight mass with them; it moved me, so I believed in their God. After being whisked away secretly from my grandparents, I lost all my faith. The loud-mouth preachers that ranted to us in the prisons did nothing but totally irritate me. My grandparents' God was not the cruel judge these preachers claimed would condemn me if I didn't straighten up.

I didn't touch that Bible for a day or two, then decided to read it, just so I could say "I've read the Bible." I laid it on the floor next to my bunk so it wouldn't fall apart, and opened to the beginning.

I started … *"Genesis, Chapter One..."* Reading it was very hard for me, not because I couldn't read well but because of the heavy medication I was still on. My mind jumped back and forth between my crime and the words on the Bible pages. I kept reading, hoping to find answers about how I'd ended up here.

I had no direction in my life, so why did it matter where I ended up? I never mattered to Mom or my stepdads. Only to my grandparents, Otto and Nellie, who had showed me a life so different than what I'd experienced. Then Mom had snatched me away from them.

Why do I blame myself for what Mom did (or didn't) do? When I left home at sixteen, why did it matter what I did? No one cared and I had to survive somehow on my own. Except once in a while it did matter what I did. Like when I hurt the boss who had co-signed for the car I wrecked and left in the desert. That was wrong…

Now, here I am, sitting in jail. I didn't even know the Rodericks. *They'd never hurt me like my stepdads did. So why did I kill them? That was wrong, too, but I can't undo it. I can't ask their forgiveness. No one else can forgive me either.* As I read the Bible, slowly I had many questions. When the sergeant came, I'd ask him to explain something.

I'd been out of touch with the Dankers for a long time; my own fault. Lois still wrote, in spite of what I'd done. She and Frederick never gave up on me. I wrote her that I was reading a Bible, but confused. She suggested I start with the first New Testament book written by Matthew.

The first sentence of Matthew was a big sign to me! *"The book of the generation / of Jesus Christ, / the Son of David, / the Son of Abraham."* It was divided into four parts evenly and I was still transfixed by groups of "fours." Matthew also wrote about Jesus, so I read more.

I still didn't understand much with my mixed-up drugged mind. I did understand, "Thou shall not kill" and "Whosoever shall kill shall be in danger of the judgment." Then I read in the next verse that even if someone is angry with another person without a good reason, he's equally guilty and subject to the same judgment. I was guilty on all counts.

Matthew also said I could be forgiven. I wanted to believe that, but couldn't. I was charged with the worst crime a man could commit. These words apply to others, but not me. My guilt wouldn't let me believe it or accept the words, yet I couldn't stop reading. I found John 3:16 "For God so loved the world that he gave his only begotten son, so *whosoever* believeth in him should not perish, but have everlasting life." *Am I a "whosoever?"*

It was just too much to accept; my sin was too great. *Can God forgive me, even if people can't? Could Jesus love me?* I'd wanted love all my life. I understood Jesus' sadness about my sins and started slowly to feel his love.

Late one night, I found the crucifixion story in Luke. I knew that Jesus had been crucified but never thought about what he went through, suffering for many hours. *Jesus, you died so that I could live!* All of a sudden I couldn't hold back my tears. I got down on my knees on the hard cement floor in my jail cell. I didn't know how to pray, but I remembered reading the Lord's Prayer so found and read it out loud. I began to talk to God about what I'd been reading.

I'd always pictured God as a judge who destroyed men, women and children when they were disobedient. But I felt a lot of love for Jesus, and on my knees in that cell, I asked for his forgiveness and peace inside. I asked his help to get my life set right for a change. I asked for an end to chronic loneliness, something I'd lived with every day of my life. And, regardless of what happened to me and no matter where I would go, I asked Jesus to help me finally grow up and mature. *Most of all, Jesus, teach me to love and care about others.* I fell asleep praying.

I spent the following days pacing my cell, reading the bible, trying to understand it all. The old gospel song, *Just a Closer Walk with Thee*, kept going around and around in my mind.

I still had many questions so the sergeant asked if I'd like to talk to his pastor. Pastor Larry Settle dropped by the jail the next day. He was pleasant, friendly and soft-spoken. I liked and trusted him right away. He had a busy life, but visited me, answered my questions and never rushed to leave. He said I could have complete forgiveness and eternal life with the Lord Jesus—me, a man sitting in jail, accused of murder! It was hard to believe but I held on to hope. I had the greatest gift in my life. I was a new man and was ready to face my fate...

Sentencing: Arraignment, Judge Robert Campbell, February 9, 1974

My trial was scheduled. I could have fought my charges all the way, but I was through fighting. I'd fought and struck out all my life, at everything and everyone. Fighting never brought me anything but heartache, loneliness and pain. No more! Certainly, the life I'd led and the things I'd done didn't leave me deserving any kind of break in the least.

My attorney, O'Connor, waived a trial by jury. He didn't think I was emotionally up to a trial.

New in my faith and filled with remorse, I didn't want the community to have to spend $50,000 for court and trial costs after what I'd already done and had cost them. Regardless of what happened to me in the future, I decided I would live through it by studying God's word and trusting in his promises. I made a decision: I told my attorney that I wished to plead guilty to the murder charges.

I'd originally been charged with first degree murder (which in Michigan was an automatic life sentence.) Because I agreed to forgo a trial, my charge was changed to second degree murder (allowing me to be paroled in the future).

On February 9, 1974 I officially pled guilty to "Second degree murder."

It would have been better for me to have fought my case and then hope for a legal issue later. The judge intended to sentence me to a lesser sentence. However, it was election time and the new prosecutor was out to look good. I remember his assistant sitting with me in my jail cell, telling me, "We really hate sending you to prison, but there's just nowhere else to send you. Plead guilty to the second and you'll be out in ten years." I was still on strong medications and so doped up and passive about everything, I went right along with it. There was no way to prove that discussion later.

Sentencing, Judge Robert Campbell, March 1, 1974

So, instead of a trial, I went to the courtroom and pled guilty to the charges. God was surely with me then! The court decided that I would be sentenced under only one charge. This is what the prosecutor had agreed to. A second-degree charge meant I was legally eligible for parole after ten years. I say God was with me, because I *could* have been sentenced under three separate charges for killing the man, his wife, and their unborn child. Or even first-degree charges, meaning I'd spend the rest of my natural life in prison and never be released.

Someone in the court suggested a sentence of 40 to 60 years (with parole possible after 15 years) but O'Connor argued for a life sentence with a minimum of 10 years instead, thinking I could be released earlier.

Judge Campbell sentenced me. The judge sat at his bench and also told me, "You keep a clean institutional record, Robert, and by law you can be out in ten years." What he told me did not appear in my legal papers, nor did he know then that the policy of the Michigan Department of Corrections (MDOC) and parole board would change drastically a few years later...

However, at that point, I had only one big concern.

In my Bible reading at the county jail cell, I read that I should be baptized. Though at the time I didn't fully understand it, I decided I needed to be baptized. But I was in jail, on my way to prison, so how? I talked with Pastor Settle and cried because I thought it was hopeless. The next time he came to see me, he told me not to say anything and that he was working something out.

When March fourth came for my trip to prison, I had a surprise. The pastor and Sergeant Parrish were driving me to the prison. On the way, we stopped at their church. Pastor Settle pointed me to the baptismal clothes laid out for me. There I was baptized in their baptismal tank and very happy. As we continued on our way, going to prison didn't seem to matter. I arrived at the prison with my hair still wet.

The maximum security prison in Jackson, Michigan was massive, cold and ominous. The thought of going inside didn't bother me much. I knew that God was in control of my life and would watch out for me. I had a true sense of peace for the first time in my life. I wasn't worried, knew that Jesus was with me, so I would be fine.

Jackson (State Prison of Southern Michigan)

1974

I became resident #137462 of the Michigan Department of Corrections (MDOC), at the Jackson Reception Diagnostic Center inside the State Prison of Southern Michigan (SPSM), better known then as "Jackson, max."

I saw a psychologist and told him I was tense and unable to sleep because I was taken suddenly off all my medication. He agreed I still needed it and put this report into my file:

CRO—109
REV. 10/73

MICHIGAN DEPARTMENT OF CORRECTIONS

RECEPTION DIAGNOSTIC CENTER

PSYCHOLOGICAL REPORT

NAME		NUMBER	INTERVIEW DATE	
BRYAN, Robert		A-137462	March 11, 1974	
OFFENSE		TERM		AGE
Murder 2nd		Life		36

TESTS ADMINISTERED:
- ☒ BETA, S.A.T., M.M.P.I., I.S.B., B.G., D.A.P., B.P.I., S.T.E.A.
- ☐ BETA, W.A.I.S., W.R.A., B.G., D.A.P., S.T.E.A.
- ☐ CLINICAL INTERVIEW
- ☐ OTHER: (   ).

INTELLECTUAL EVALUATION: This man scored to have superior intelligence, IQ 124, grade level 10.5.

LEARNING POTENTIAL: This man has learned how to receive help, at the Forensic Center where he has been medicated for about a year and he has learned now, that by asking for help, he may possibly receive medication again.

PSYCHODYNAMICS: Robert seems to be in a relative contact with reality, at this time, that allows him to be coherent. This man states that he has been under a great deal of tension this past week and has not been able to sleep, due to the fact that he was on heavy medication for about a year at the Forensic Center and has not had help since being here.

Robert's discomfort, agitation and tension did not allow this examiner to pursue etiological dynamics. Robert was able to volunteer for and went to the Reform Program, at age 18 in Missouri, and that he has served time in Nevada and in Mississippi and indicates his latest release was 10-19-68.

ETIOLOGY OF CRIMINAL BEHAVIOR: This man indicates that in March of 1972, he lost his job and he was afraid he was going to lose his wife and he just took off driving and had what he would call a complete nervous breakdown. This led to the current charge and no details were discussed at that time, but it did involve murder.

PROGNOSIS: Robert is probably not going to be able to handle a regular program, without a great deal of medication, or without special psychiatric support.

PROGRAM RECOMMENDATIONS: This man's disturbance, his needs for tranquilizing medication and the possibility of depressive suicidal or assaultive qualities, would tend to suggest he should be moved, as an emergency Top Six, and will be taken there immediately by this examiner. This man was written in as a member of the psychiatric clinic, immediately under the direction of Dr. Pesetsky.

M. J. Keyser, Clinical Psychologist

Top Six

I was back on medication and housed in 'Top Six,' the highest security level. When I saw the psychologist again, he decided to wean me off all the medications gradually. Instead, the staff took me off all at once. I couldn't sleep, sit or stand

58

still. I paced back and forth in my cell day and night, walking and praying, asking the Lord for relief.

I was assigned a public defender from the Michigan Court of Appeals but wasn't sure if anyone could help. This is the report that that attorney later gave:

> I visited Mr. Bryan at Jackson Prison in 1974 and found him to be exclusively preoccupied with controlling his emotional state. He had only recently begun withdrawal from the massive doses of tranquilizing drugs prescribed for him at the Forensic Center and at Jackson. He was withdrawn and his hand shook visibly. He expressed uncertainty about desiring post-conviction relief. He was able to recall few of the facts necessary for preparation of his case, and the discomfort caused him to be unable to discuss his case.
>
> B. Levine, State Appellate Defender

Finally I was well enough to move to Level 5, maximum security.[1]

About one fourth of the SPSM yard   *Inside 5 block*

---

[1] The Michigan prison system classified prisons and inmates by how much security was needed based on risk factors (considering the crime, escape potential and behavior in the prison system). The higher the level number, the higher the risk. Some prisons had more than one security level, allowing those with a lower classification more privileges and freedom to move within the same prison walls.

Level 5

The prison was huge; it held over 5,000 inmates on 3,500 acres. There was a 34-foot-high concrete wall stretching around the entire prison. Twelve watch towers, sixteen cellblocks. All the cells are ten feet long, by six feet wide, by seven and a half feet high. This would be my home for a long time…

Dining hall   *Row of cells*   *Five stories*

My cell was on the second tier of five, in the very end. Behind my cell was a walkway, with my cell open both in front and in back so anyone on the walkway could reach almost anything in it. Two days after getting there, someone reached in and stole some of my things. I told the officer that I wanted a change. The officer told me I'd better get back to my cell or he'd write me up. I asked to see the captain, who agreed to transfer me to another cell. I was still in a maximum security prison, but my new cell was safer.

Maximum security is the roughest place to be, and I had to watch my back all the time. Inmates carefully check out and challenge new arrivals to see if they are strong and will defend themselves or can be used as their slaves, their girlfriends or as a warrior in their gang. Of all these roles, the girlfriend one—sexual abuse—was what I feared the most. Many of the men were also abused as children and became abusers themselves. I did not want my experience with Dale ever repeated. I was grateful I'd learned to defend myself.

I started to work on my GED. As well as my school books, I dug into my Bible. Proverbs was the best textbook I'd ever read on how to live as a Christian man. One of my favorite verses was Proverbs 3:5-7, "Trust in the LORD with all your heart, and lean not on your own understanding; in all your ways acknowledge him, and he shall direct your paths. Do not be wise in your own eyes; fear the LORD and depart from evil."

In prison, without real friends yet, I had to trust God to protect me. You either become better or worse when in prison. I wanted to be better and Jesus slowly changed me. I'd hated my mother; but that feeling left me. I couldn't say I loved Mom or wanted to see her, but my bitterness was gone. God not only protected me, he taught me to be a different kind of man. The psychiatrists had said I'd never be free of my mental illness, but they didn't know about the healing that Jesus could do.

1975

As a kid, I was called Bob, but hated it when Mom called me in, she pronounced it *Baby* instead of *Bobby* in front of my friends. I'd loved my grandfather Otto, so I told everyone in the prison my name was Otto (which was my middle name). I was a new man who needed a new name!

After my public defender, Levine, withdrew because of her large caseload, Attorney Dereck Carter was assigned my case. I wanted to get my sentence reduced from "twenty to life" to a number of years. I thought that's what my trial attorney, O'Connor, should have insisted on. Carter was young and inexperienced, but I liked him and felt he was on my side.

During my first year at Jackson, I didn't have any visitors but did get letters from Lois Danker and Pastor Settle. My prison world began to expand when I got letters from a Christian family in western Michigan, Ruby, Al and their daughter, Connie. They were friends of another inmate and began writing me too. They were the first folks to visit when I was lonelier than I'd ever been before.

It didn't take me long to complete high school studies. I earned my GED diploma in less than a year and was re-classified as a Level 4. Done with my academic classes, I started painting again. My first painting was of three kittens playing with a ball of twine. It wasn't outstanding, but I sold

61

it for enough to order more art materials. Most of my earlier art went to the Dankers to sell or give to their friends. The Dankers had set aside and saved the disability payments I got while at the Forensic center, plus the money for the artwork they sold for me.

I decided to begin a journal of my days in prison…

~

November I spent all my spare time on artwork in my small cell until we got an art teacher, Tom Rudd. I liked Tom and he requested me as his assistant. I didn't get paid, but I got to use some of the materials and learned a lot as Rudd taught the other inmates. My artwork had always brought me the positive attention that I missed growing up.

Tom was a sculptor, so I decided to try that. One of my first pieces was just for fun–maybe in bad taste–but still fun! I made a hefty gal about eighteen inches tall and named her *Big Bertha*. I told the guys in the class that a man needs a woman like Bertha to keep warm in the winter.

December Tom Rudd arranged a prison art exhibit for us at Siena Heights College in Adrian and I was busy with that. I also did some Christian artwork for a show the Dankers were setting up at the seminary in St. Louis next year, and they planned to drive to Michigan to pick up all the work I had ready. Besides paintings, I'd carved linoleum blocks and made prints from them.

I had so many pieces of art that I ran out of storage space, so my buddy Mick offered his cell. He enjoyed having it and it freed up my space. Because of my art, I had a good reputation among the prison employees. I minded my own business and didn't get into trouble and that positive attention was therapeutic for me. If I didn't have something productive to do, I'd be depressed about being in prison.

1976

January I got an interesting letter from a woman, Diane Russell. One of my friends in the art class who was recently released from SPSM told her about me. I didn't know then, but my whole life would change. She was interested in seeing my work. She was divorced, with two children, had been an art teacher and left teaching to work for IBM, repairing equipment in Detroit.

In my reply, I told her about the prison art exhibit at Siena Heights College, where I'd entered some paintings, prints and an abstract sculpture. Diane and a friend went to see it and she wrote again, a longer letter this time. She wanted to hear about other artwork I'd done and what I was working on. In her letters, Diane came across as a strong-but-warm woman who was adamant about women's rights.

Some of my artwork at the Siena Heights Exhibit

March Other people wrote me about my art at the exhibit too. One letter was an invitation to show my work in a brand new Eclectic Gallery scheduled to open in the Adrian Mall. The art gallery owner, a friend of Rudd's and an artist himself, saw my paintings at Siena Heights and wanted a one-man show in his gallery. I could hardly believe he chose my work!

By the end of the month, I was angry. I hadn't received any money for my things that sold at the art show or those the Dankers had sold. I had no money to buy more art supplies and was frustrated that I had to depend on others for what I'd needed my whole life! Even the Eclectic art gallery offer fell through; Tom's friend didn't have enough money to open.

My anger didn't last; I soon got excited again about doing a prison cell assemblage, a painting using actual items. I planned to make a four-by-seven foot board, to be viewed

63

from both sides. The electrical department foreman promised me fixtures and wiring, and plumbing friends offered a sink and pipes. I'd supply the plywood, a frame, the acrylic paint and medium to hold it all together. I wrote my new friend, Diane, about it and sent her a sketch.

April The Dankers came to Michigan, picked up my art for the next St. Louis show, and then I didn't do anything but lie around listening to music, drinking coffee and thinking. I cleaned my cell from one end to the other. I needed more money so wrote the Dankers. They'd banked it, rather than sending it to me. Lois said that I'd need that money when I'm released.

Money had been a problem for me all my life; prison pay was very low and I had to plan weeks ahead to order supplies, then find a way to pay for them before I could finish and sell another piece of art.

My good friend Doc and I did a lot of work to get a *Prison Arts* magazine going. Inmates wrote stories and poetry, I did several drawings to illustrate their stories and we battled with the prison administration to print it.

My artwork for Prison Arts Magazine

Doc's cell was across from mine and he also painted. He was very smart, always had answers and was good at working angles to get what we needed. I couldn't order modeling paste for my paintings, so Doc got me some patching plaster from the maintenance crew and I mixed it with acrylic medium and started to work on my prison assemblage.

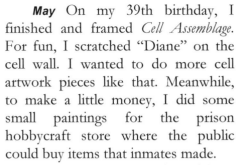

May On my 39th birthday, I finished and framed *Cell Assemblage*. For fun, I scratched "Diane" on the cell wall. I wanted to do more cell artwork pieces like that. Meanwhile, to make a little money, I did some small paintings for the prison hobbycraft store where the public could buy items that inmates made.

Next, I started a series of large paintings showing how hollow people are without God in their lives. The first was a hollow man with small hollow figures crawling inside him. I called the series *Man Without God.*

My estranged wife, Kay, filed for divorce. We'd exchanged a few letters in the last four years, but she never

Man Without God: #101, #203, #204

came to see me. Our marriage was really over when I left St. Louis.

My new friend, Diane, planned to come visit me and I was as nervous as a teenager on a first date. However, the visit didn't happen. We were allowed four visits a month, and I'd used mine for visits with friends I'd met through other inmates. Diane arrived to learn she couldn't visit until next month. I called her to apologize and was afraid that she might never come again.

June Diane did come again and I didn't act like a stupid teenager. We talked easily and enjoyed getting to know each other. She came a third time and we talked even more. She mailed me a photo of herself with her two children. I wished I been part of a family like hers. If I had, I wouldn't have been in prison.

July On Diane's next visit, she told me she had a chance for a job with IBM in North Carolina. We were just getting to know each other. If she moved, would I ever see her again?

A prisoner tried to escape down a rope through his cell window, so guards tore all our cells apart, looking for things we might use to escape. One guard came into my cell, but instead of tearing it up, he stood and looked at my artwork on the walls. He gave one light tap on the window to ensure it wouldn't open, then left.

The summer heat took its toll–stabbings, beatings, pipe bombs, inmates walking off their jobs in some sort of protest or another. I didn't have the energy to do any artwork.

Tom told me that the Eclectic gallery was going to open after all in the fall and still wanted to go ahead with my one-man show. So, in spite of the heat, I started painting.

August Diane brought her daughter for a visit and I enjoyed meeting Chandra, a thirteen-year old who giggled a lot. Diane's North Carolina job fell through, but she said she'd be flying to New York for an interview as a technical writer. I was happy she had this second chance, but at the same time, everything inside me screamed, *No, Diane, you can't go!* On our next visit, I kissed Diane goodbye for the first time. I wondered if I'd ever see her again if she moved to New York.

Our visiting room was small and crowded, but inmates and their visitors were so wrapped up with each other, we didn't pay much attention to anyone else. Diane and I joked, talked about art and our lives and feelings. She made me feel that I was capable, intelligent and talented.

I got a letter from Evelyne Porter who lived in the city of Jackson; she and her husband Bob wanted to visit me. I replied that I was always glad to make new friends. I was delighted when I met them, such a happy, loving couple.

I painted the largest picture in my *Man Without God* series, *#202,* and also started a new series, *Forgotten Wishes.* We all make wishes and most don't come true. What happens to those we forget about? They must be out there, somewhere, maybe in a lonely empty space, just hanging or laying around. I put those wishbones in my paintings.

Man without God #202

Forgotten Wishes

Doc and I often discussed art. He copied landscapes but couldn't paint anything original. I told him to paint what he saw in his mind, and he said that he saw numbers or words. In my mind, I saw images, and told him that I couldn't paint a picture with words.

Three pieces of my art were in Lansing for a show, and the Pontiac Creative Arts Center planned a prisoner art show in the fall. I promised Tom I'd finish as much artwork as I could for it. Tom had recently been in New York City checking out art galleries and said my work would sell very well there.

Some of my calender prints

To have more pieces to sell at exhibits, I carved linoleum blocks and made prints. I sent copies of each of my Bible prints to Diane. I designed twelve different blocks, thinking they might be used for a twelve-month calendar some day.

Diane was training another woman as her replacement in Detroit to repair IBM equipment, because she was going to Poughkeepsie (in eastern New York), on a temporary assignment as a technical writer. I gave her a fun painting I did of a necklace she'd made, hanging it from a toilet float instead of her neck. I also gave her one of my *Forgotten Wishes* paintings and a photo of me. I wanted her walls in Poughkeepsie so full of my art that she couldn't forget about me.

Toilet Float　　　*Hanging Wishes*　　　*Otto, 1976*

September Diane and Chandra moved to an apartment in Poughkeepsie. Her son, Kris, moved into his father and stepmother's house in Michigan.

I'd miss Diane, so was glad to be busy getting ready for art shows. I made a print, *YHWH*, which is the Jewish name for God, Yahweh (ancient Hebrew didn't have vowels). I liked the way the letters hooked together. Eclectic Gallery sent out an invitation to my one-man exhibit.

I also did simple child-like paintings, *The Lost Sheep* and *Jonah and the Whale*.

YHWH print　　　*The Lost Sheep*　　　*Jonah and the Whale*

Diane wrote that she'd drive back to Michigan for my Eclectic show. She was clearly out of my league, smart, well-educated with an excellent job. She inspired me to succeed and set goals, and I wanted to make her proud of me.

She asked about my sentence. I told her I could be released in ten to fifteen years if my public defender got me resentenced. Occasionally, men and women were released early on a 'special parole' for outstanding behavior, but I couldn't count on that.

Diane enjoyed her writing job in Poughkeepsie far more than repair work. I missed her, but couldn't ask her to return to Michigan; she had to do what was best for her and her children. What I could do was work hard to be released from prison so that–if she wished–I could move closer to her.

My friend Mick was overjoyed that Chandra wrote to him; she also wrote some of my other friends. I was so proud of her, a young teenager, taking her time to bring us some happiness.

October I got my final divorce papers from Kay, glad that she could move on to a better life than I'd given her. Diane still had doubts about our future. I was afraid I'd lose her to another man before I got out.

November While Diane was back in Michigan, she met my new friends, the Porters. She and the Porters saw my one-man show at Eclectic together as it was being set up.

I worked steadily on my art for a St. Louis show in a few months. My paintings were again stored in my friend Mick's cell because I had no more space in mine. He said he enjoyed living in my art gallery.

Diane wrote that while telling me some of her problems, my face looked like Jesus' face because I'd showed her so much kindness and compassion. I replied that I was in prison because I was *not* good and certainly not like Jesus. I'd grown up angry and hurt others badly, but God was changing me. Diane started asking more questions about faith in her letters and about why I was so content, living in prison. I didn't push Christianity on her; it had always made me angry when someone did that to me.

I wrote her that my relationship with God was like a friendship that happened over time. I did not understand the

69

father, son and holy spirit thing at all. In fact, a father was someone I feared and hid from. But Jesus? Jesus was pure love and compassion. He even sacrificed himself for me! I became his friend first. Then he introduced me to his father and the holy spirit. Jesus showed me that not all fathers were like my stepfathers had been. Because I loved Jesus, God the father loved me too. So did his spirit, who became my teacher and guide.

As evil as my past actions were, God still loved me–and his love never ceased to amaze me. That love filled up the old empty Otto, so it could overflow to others. I finally had a father who loved and protected me, especially in a dangerous place like prison.

December Bad news for me; my friend Doc would be transferred to a trustee prison, where he'd have more privileges. It was a step toward his release, but he and

Michael   Doc   Otto

I were a good team and he didn't want to go to trustee. I still had my closest friend, Michael, who was the brother I'd always wanted.

I hadn't told Diane much about my past, other than since I'd met Jesus, my life was never the same. She believed I was a new man and said that's what mattered. Maybe later I could tell her my whole story, but not then. We wrote long letters to each other, sometimes several a week.

Good news from Lois Danker; my paintings and prints sold in St. Louis for over $1,500. Lois had already booked me for an April showing. A church in Lansing also wanted my work for their June show.

My friend Doc and I packed his belongings as we said goodbye and he left for trustee. He promised to stay in touch with me.

Diane sent several of my friends her hand-made Christmas cards. Michael was especially pleased because he rarely got mail. Michael was my closest friend and like Doc, he was very smart, we trusted each other and we talked over everything.

On Christmas day Diane came to visit. Even a short visit with her, holding her hand, was great. She went to the Porters after our visit. They had picked up my Christmas gift for her, a painting, *Memories of Diane,* where I'd added some of her actual letters.

I hated to end visits, not only because it meant separating from friends but also because of the body searches we had to endure, baring our private parts for a guard's inspection. It took me back to memories of Dale and I felt violated again each time.

1977

January I redid my cell to make it into my own personal studio, with my drawing board in one corner and a shade so my ceiling light shone on my artwork on the walls. I hung my drawing tools on one wall and my artwork where I could easily change it. I had a lot of things in a six by ten-foot space! It looked cluttered but was very organized for work.

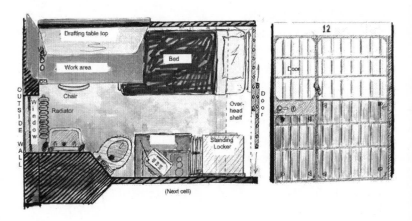

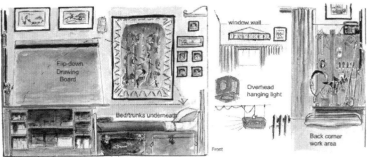

Life was very cheap in prison. A man could get killed by mistake if he was in the wrong place at the wrong time. If you didn't want to kill someone yourself, you could buy it done with cigarettes or a little money. To stay alive, you had to let others know you could take care of yourself, if necessary.

A lot went on that I never told my visitors about. I especially hated to talk about my background, even to inmates who may have done worse crimes than mine. I still felt ashamed for taking three lives that I couldn't give back.

February Diane wrote that she was asking an IBM co-worker questions about Christianity.

March I had a visit with a man who had a small Christian printing business in Michigan. He'd seen some of my artwork and prints, so offered me a job when I was released. People believed in me, and that always surprised me.

Diane accepted a permanent writing job in New York. I was proud of her, but also worried that some man there would snatch her up. I didn't have anything to offer her except my love and didn't want to lose her before I got out of prison.

April I met Diane's son, Kris, for the first time and liked him. He told me Diane was buying a house in Poughkeepsie.

July I got the best news of my life–my prayers were answered. Because we couldn't get phone calls from outside the prison, Diane's co-worker sent me a mailgram to tell me that Diane had said "yes" to Jesus!

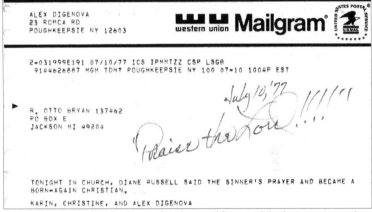

ALEX DIGENOVA
23 ROMCA RD
POUGHKEEPSIE NY 12603

western union **Mailgram**

2-031999E191 07/10/77 ICS IPMMTZZ CSP LSGB
9144626887 MGM TDMT POUGHKEEPSIE NY 100 07-10 1004P EST

R. OTTO BRYAN 137462
PO BOX E
JACKSON MI 49204

July 10, '77

TONIGHT IN CHURCH, DIANE RUSSELL SAID THE SINNER'S PRAYER AND BECAME A BORN-AGAIN CHRISTIAN.

KARIN, CHRISTINE, AND ALEX DIGENOVA

I knew her whole outlook on life would change, as mine had. She hadn't lived a bad life like me, but I knew she'd be happier. I could handle anything that came along, knowing that we'd both be in heaven for eternity. I wrote to Diane:

73

Diane was the only woman I'd ever truly loved. She'd helped me become a different person; certainly a much happier one. Even if I never got out of prison, I'd always thank Jesus for her friendship and love. On our visits we sometimes disagreed but never left angry at one another. We shared more of our feelings in letters and both missed each other between visits.

My court action was more important to me since I'd met Diane and had a reason to leave prison. My attorney, Carter, told me he was still waiting for some court documents, then would fight my original sentence because of my mental state at the time of sentencing. Morally, I wasn't sure if I should fight my sentence.

September I decided Diane should know about my crime so she'd understand me better. I couldn't tell her myself, so suggested she read a book by Dr. Tanay, who had interviewed me while I was at the Forensic center. He'd published a book about some of his cases, *The Murderers*. My story was the first one. I couldn't tell him what went on inside of me when I killed the Rodericks, so he based my story on newspaper accounts and guessed at what he didn't know.

October Diane started reading *The Murderers* while I fasted and prayed for days. So much was going through my mind! Would I lose her? I stayed buried in my Bible and begged God to give her the faith to realize that He had turned the Otto of the past into the new man she knew. I wrote her:

    I keep asking God to give your faith all
    the strength he possibly can, to let you
    see that the Otto you've seen in the past
    two years is absolutely sincere and not the
    one you read about.

    Sweetheart, it's no different for me.
    How many times have I told you that it just
    makes me sick to think about the things in
    my past? You said it is a different man you
    read about? Don't you think I have the same
    feeling?

Because it is in my past, the only chance I have of even keeping my sanity is by staying close to Jesus. Is it really a wonder to you that I'm no longer bitter? Look what Christ has done in my life, despite the life I once led. God gave me peace and removed my overwhelming guilt. But Christ didn't stop there. Just look at all the tremendous blessings he's showered on me! Can there really be any wonder why I love now, rather than hate? Only the wondrous power of God did that. Some high-priced psychiatrist can't do it … and unless the psychiatrist knows the power of Christ, he couldn't even understand it!

November Diane didn't give up on me and I thanked Jesus over and over. I knew I could handle anything that might come along. After a Thanksgiving trip to Michigan, Diane sent me a mailgram. I drew my reply on it and mailed it back to her.

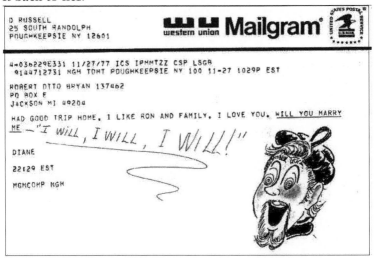

D RUSSELL
25 SOUTH RANDOLPH
POUGHKEEPSIE NY 12601

western union **Mailgram**

4-036229E331 11/27/77 ICS IPMMTZZ CSP LSGB
9144712731 MGM TDMT POUGHKEEPSIE NY 100 11-27 1029P EST

ROBERT OTTO BRYAN 137462
PO BOX E
JACKSON MI 49204

HAD GOOD TRIP HOME. I LIKE RON AND FAMILY. I LOVE YOU. WILL YOU MARRY
ME — "I WILL, I WILL, I WILL!"

DIANE

22129 EST

MGMCOMP MGM

She really wanted to marry me, knowing my background? Was she strong enough to stick with me? I already owed her more than I could ever repay. No one but me really understood the hatred, loneliness, and bitterness that used to rule every minute of my life. I hated my father for deserting

75

us, my mother for neglecting me, my stepfathers for abusing me, the juvenile home and prisons, the police, everyone. I thanked God that little of that old hatred remained. I wasn't ready to forgive Dale yet.

December My new attorney, Carter, sent me a copy of his court brief and wrote he expected a denial, but it was just the first step. He said I might have to go through the state supreme court about my mental health issue.

Some of my art sold for over $1,000 at the Pontiac art show. I got $680 and the exhibitors got the rest for their expenses. My large cell assemblage was out on loan somewhere. A film crew came to interview me and were allowed right into my cell to film while we chatted about art. Tom had left the prison to work on his own sculptures and our art program ended, along with my job. I wasn't sure I could continue with my art.

On Christmas Day, Diane, Chandra and Kris visited me. As a kid, Mom and I had never celebrated Christmas but now I had a real reason to celebrate Jesus' birth.

1978

Otto at Varitype Machine

Spectator Editorial cartoon

January I went to work on the staff of the weekly prison newspaper, the *Spectator*. I did typesetting and occasional artwork.

Our editor was transferred to another prison and without his supervision, the office became a dope, gambling and sex hangout because we had solid walls and the guards didn't see what was going on as they walked by. It was hard for us to work because too many men crowded in. Before long, we had a big shakedown and guards came in to find needles, syringes, pot and betting stubs. I was glad I wasn't there when they came–or I might have gone to the hole too. Because of my earlier extreme loneliness, I was still afraid I'd fall apart mentally or kill myself if I were cut off from everyone again in the hole.

Diane wrote again that she was serious about marriage! She told me that in a church service, the guest evangelist had said, "If God tells you to do something, do it!" At that moment, Diane heard the holy spirt whisper to her, 'Marry Otto.' A few days later she asked a Christian friend at work how to know God's will and he told her, "You just know it." So she knew she should marry me. Neither of us had any idea then what her decision would mean for us.

She joked we should get married on May 7 (my forty-first birthday) because she didn't know what else to give me for a birthday gift. Besides, she told me, I wouldn't ever forget our anniversary. I was overwhelmed with happiness, so any date was fine with me. I walked down to see Michael in a daze and asked him to be best man. My mind was whirling; I loved her so much! I'd never known anyone who inspired and encouraged me like she did.

I agreed to take on the job as *Spectator* editor, because the supervisors said I could use a small room in the office to do my artwork. But I had no time for art, only getting the paper out. I oversaw everything and everyone, wrote editorials, did all the typesetting and some drawings for the paper.

I "starred" in another short movie that pointed out the negatives of prison life for an artist. The cameramen took pictures of my cell while other inmates joked that I should get them walk-on parts. It took two days to record the twenty-minute film.

February My friend Michael went to the hospital in Jackson because of his diabetes and heart problems. I worried about him because he was my closest friend ever.

On Valentine's Day, Diane sent me a card saying she was serious about marriage. Her sister Sharon told Diane our getting married was dumb. Other than the kids, I hadn't written or met any of her family yet.

My attorney, Carter, wrote he hoped to hold my hearing later in the month. He believed the judge and the prosecutor would be fair about my appeal. Diane knew I was frustrated and impatient with the lack of progress and wrote that if I wanted to hire an attorney, she'd pay for one. I couldn't accept, but was touched and thankful for her offer.

March Our *Spectator* office turned into a poker parlor again; the last big shakedown hadn't helped. We had no space to work. I only had authority over the office staff, not others who crowded in. I couldn't snitch or I'd be killed, so I simply walked off the job.

Michael got back from the hospital, and I was very glad to see him well again.

I was recruited to work with the prison JOLT program, where young felons came in to discover what life in prison was really like. My role was to tape record the sessions and design a logo for them. We had our first JOLT tour and it went well. The boys came in cocky, but didn't leave that way! We locked them up and let some of the worst inmates have fun taunting them as if they were fine young girls and what they'd like to do with them sexually. Within thirty minutes, all the kids were shaking.

Weddings in SPSM were held in the small parole interview room. After a simple ceremony, the wedding party could have a group visit. I'd never written Diane's folks and thought I should. I wanted to let them know how much I loved her and the kids.

Chandra wrote me that if I made her Mom happy, she'd be happy too. She asked me to promise I'd never hurt her or Diane. How could I? I loved them both too much.

It was difficult getting married in prison. I had to sign up

78

for the prison chaplain's group talk, get a blood test and send the certificate to Diane so she could apply for our license. I also had to give Chaplain Saunders copies of my divorce papers and send a copy to Diane too. We were allowed only ten wedding guests, half of them inmates, so I invited Michael and four of my friends. I told the chaplain we wanted Pastor Settle to officiate. I wrote the pastor to arrange the date for May 7th. Diane had to present all our paperwork to the Jackson County clerk to issue a license. I hoped the county clerk would waive the seven-day waiting period so Diane didn't have to make two trips to Michigan.

 We wanted unique wedding rings, so I designed them: plain gold bands with two interlocking circles and a cross in the center. Diane found a jeweler in Poughkeepsie who made them. The thought of wearing that ring thrilled me. *April* I wrote a letter to Diane's folks; they replied:

```
Dear Otto:
Ella and I are answering your letter of
April 14 separately. Otherwise neither
could be honest.
I really do not know you and I have
trouble understanding those I know well.
I love her greatly. Yet I cannot
understand her differing moods. Sometimes
her decisions seem very erratic to me. At
times she is highly intelligent and
logical. At times, she is both impulsive
and impractical.
Her sudden plans to get married the
first time completely surprised me. She was
away at school and I had not noticed the
changes in her attitude and goals.
That marriage was a disaster. Neither
she, nor her husband, were really ready for
marriage. Apparently, they had not known
each other long. Except that they were of
about the same age and were both attending
college, they had little in common. They
both tried hard, for the children's' sake,
```

to maintain the marriage. Yet, I doubt it was ever a comfortable, loving marriage.

I cannot understand why she wants to marry again under the present circumstances.

The little I know of you has been gained from a few letters, from samples of your art, and a very little from second and third hand information.

Your letters are very intense, serious and apparently considerate. They show a deep religious faith and complete trust in Christ. They indicate an acceptance of your situation without resentment or hatred. They show full acceptance of Christ who promises both eternal salvation and forgiveness of sins.

I cannot advise, much less tell, you and Diane what to do, nor when to do it. I can assure you that if you obtain a parole, I will do everything I can to help you during the very difficult times that will follow.

Please ask yourself if it would not be better for you and Diane to wait until you are released and reestablished in society. She might not stand the strains and possible disappointments that will certainly occur.

Yours in Christ, Harry W. Russell

April 20, 1978
Dear Otto

I've never had any doubts about your love, sincerity or admiration for Diane-nor hers for you. You have much in common thru your mutual love for art and this is all in your favor under normal circumstances.

However I do question the advantages of marriage at this point. Your times together have been so brief. Do you really know one another? Diane is normally loving & cheerful; she can also be cross, impatient and moody! (Goodies inherited from her mother?)

80

I guess what I'm concerned about is Diane's ability to cope with more stress. Should your hopes for an early release be denied, what then? Diane's newfound faith may sustain her from possible disappointments & setbacks. It was not sufficient when her previous marriage broke up.

Regardless of my doubts, I do pray that our Lord Jesus will guide you both in making the right decisions always-and that he will give me the grace to accept whatever comes. I do hope we'll be able to meet soon-hopefully on Diane's next visit.

God's blessings to you-Ella Russell

May This was the second most important day of my life; the first most important was meeting Jesus in the jail cell. Diane and I were married by Pastor Settle with friends and Diane's children as witnesses. Diane also asked her children, her best friend, Menka, and the Porters to attend. I hadn't met any of Diane's other family yet. I had four friends plus Michael. We had a group visit after the wedding.

Diane visited the next day and I couldn't stop looking at and cuddling her. I was so proud that she chose me. After she left, I polished my new wedding ring over and over, just to remind myself that it was real and how God had blessed me! Our marriage was a total commitment for me, just like the one I'd made with Jesus. Diane said maybe I loved her too much, but I told her there was no such thing as too much love.

Soon after the wedding, Chandra "adopted" me. We had a standing joke that I'd adopt her through her fictitious Brookfield Adoption

81

Agency, and she sent me the "official" notification. One way or another, we were all connected for life. I was in awe that, although I did the most horrible thing in the world, God gave me the greatest gifts of my life! Not only did I meet Jesus, I also had the family I'd always longed for. I was a blessed man.

June Judge Campbell denied me a new trial (which I knew would happen, based on an in-chamber meeting). I was still bothered that I had been so heavily medicated that I passively agreed to anything my first lawyer, O'Connor, suggested. How could that make no difference in my case? My crime was terrible—no doubt about it. I was guilty, could not undo it, and didn't asked to have that record erased. All I wanted was a chance to leave prison in the future.

The Lion's group within the prison asked me to make an award sculpture. They translated books into Braille for the blind, and I used my own hand for the cast.

I made a new friend, Larry, a young man at SPSM. He was honest and trustworthy, but not a Christian. He wanted a pen pal to write him so Diane suggested Gladys, a young Christian woman she knew in Poughkeepsie.

July I had my yearly review, and the counselor asked about my activities. I told him that besides the *Spectator*, I belonged to a Christian fellowship, went to Bible studies, did artwork and worked with JOLT. He told me the parole board didn't count religious groups as activities, yet that's the only thing that I saw bring real changes to men here.

Diane sent me a tape recording of herself, talking, reading scripture and singing while playing her guitar. I listened to it over and over and imagined being home with her. We weren't allowed non-commercial tapes but could receive religious teachings, so Diane asked a friend who owned a Christian bookstore to mail it in their packaging to me.

August Diane and I continued writing long letters; it was the best way to talk between visits. I'd never been so committed to anyone before. The old Otto didn't need anyone, but I finally found someone I couldn't do without.

We finally got a *Spectator* editor who fired the guys who were not working and then we had a race issue. My young friend Larry dropped in now and then to check on us. One of the men who was fired came in with a knife and went after Larry. Larry grabbed one of the heavy varitype machines, wiring and all, and pushed it so hard against the attacker that he flew clear across the room and ran out. I was thankful God (and Larry) were on my side! Prison was definitely not a country club.

In addition to the *Spectator*, I also worked on my art. I made several sculptures of John the Baptist. After I made a mold of the basic figure, I draped clothing on additional figures made from the same mold and made several unique ones.

Diane came to Michigan for the Labor Day weekend, and I loved seeing her. I wasn't ready for marriage when I'd married Kay. My goal then was to make money so we could buy things to show off to other people. Things weren't important to me anymore; my new family was.

October I got a letter from Diane's Mom and she signed it, "*God's Blessings–Mom*." She wanted to come meet me.

Proposal B was put on the Michigan ballot stating no one could be released early until he or she had served their minimum sentence. I didn't think it was legal to apply the new law retroactively because the judges decided a sentence based on the laws in effect at the time of their sentencing.

I met more of my new family–Mom, Dad, Diane's sister Sharon, and Sharon's young son, Eric.

I especially loved Mom. She was the caring mother that

83

I'd never had; she hugged me and held my hands. Dad was a little more reserved, but also an intelligent, caring man. Sharon was quiet on that first visit, and little Eric just wanted to wrestle with me.

Dad was ready to retire and both Mom and Dad loved to travel, so that was their plan. They'd bought a large fifth wheel trailer and pickup to pull it and planned to spend their winters driving across southern USA.

November The Porter's son-in-law, who had an import business, showed some of my breadboards to a buyer for JC Penny stores. They wanted more to sell; I could hardly keep up with the demand. My friends in hobbycraft shop cut the shapes, then I wood-burned designs on them. I made Diane a small cabinet this way for Christmas too.

The prison planned to build three new rooms for officer's dining, a lounge area and a small first aid room. Deputy Grant (who had denied every request I'd made of him) asked me to draw up some rough plans for the project. "I'm an artist, not an architect," I told him, but I did as he asked.

Mom and Dad visited and bought me some Christmas treats.

Otto, Mom and Dad

December Proposal B passed. If it were retroactive, I'd get a new sentence because the judge intended that I'd get out one day. If it was not retroactive, I wasn't sure what my future would be.

I spent Christmas Day with Diane, Chandra and Kris and felt God's blessings so much. Diane came to spend New Year's Eve with me (but had to leave at nine when visiting hours were over). It was a perfect ending to the best year of my life. I finally had a real family!

1979

January I was still thinking about seeing Diane last month. She was everything I desired in a woman and wife–but of course, God knew that and planned we'd meet in the first place. I prayed she would always love me in spite of my failings. Larry and Gladys' were in love too; I laughed at Larry because he dressed up just to call Gladys on the phone.

Tensions were running high; stabbings and killings almost every day. Someone was stabbed twenty-three times in the gym, and the next day, another stabbing.

February I wrote and asked the Dankers to send my money they had set aside in my savings account to Diane to keep for me, now that she was my wife.

I talked with the counselor about my first parole hearing; he said it would be a rough one, my whole life laid open in front of the board members. I had no possibility of parole yet, so I didn't have to fret afterwards about whether I made it. At least I'd learn what to expect before my next hearing.

March That first parole board hearing was hard, listening to the details of my crime. I had walked in feeling strong and confident but as soon as they started reading my entire criminal history, I was numb. They did comment on how well I had been doing.

My new sister Sharon visited me without her boys, and we talked for three hours. She offered to call Carter to see where things stood for me.

April Diane and Chandra were in Michigan to visit. While they were here, I got a letter from forensic psychiatrist Dr. Tanay. Diane had written him after reading his book and told him how Jesus had changed me. He wanted my permission to answer her and also asked to visit me. Was it to find out if I was really different? He was part of my life I didn't want to think about; besides I'd been annoyed that he'd written his opinion about me without my permission. He had written that I'd never be emotionally well.

Carter wrote that his petition for Judge Campbell was almost ready, but first he wanted me to write about the merits of a long-term sentence over a life sentence. Then, he'd write up an affidavit, send it to me to sign and he'd present it while asking for my hearing.

We had three active Christian fellowship groups at SPSM. When I first got here, I couldn't find any. My group invited gospel singer Andrae Crouch and what a meeting we had! The next day, Pastor Louie Morabito gave a powerful message, and thirty to forty men went up for an altar call. Pastor Morabito and Frank Dimercurio came to SPSM regularly and always had a great word from God for us.

May Last night Chuck Colson spoke at SPSM. He was very committed to his Prison Fellowship ministry and signed a pocket New Testament for me to give Diane.

Our one-year anniversary came; I'd never imagined that I'd have a marriage that got better and better! It was hard for us to be separated but also a blessing because I'd never take my marriage for granted. I was just dumbfounded at God's goodness to me, that He'd blessed me with a wife I loved so deeply and a wonderful family too.

The only other people who had cared and stuck by me were the Dankers. I treasured every minute I had with any of them.

I felt bad that I didn't have anything to give Diane for our anniversary, but she simply said "Otto, you gave me the best gift in the whole world; you introduced me to Jesus!"

Whenever I struggled with my faith, I drew closer to the Lord. I didn't always get the answer I wanted.

Chandra sent me the first Father's Day card I'd ever

received and I was so touched.

Prison Fellowship held a three-day seminar here as a follow-up to Colson's visit. Diane, the Porters and other volunteers joined us for the program in our auditorium. I loved having Diane here; it felt so good to worship God next to my wife. Chuck Colson spoke on the third day and the place was packed.

I decided to mold a nail-pierced hand as a thank-you gift for Prison Fellowship. Like the Braille hand I made last year, I used my own hand for the mold.

Prison Fellowship: Michael, Diane, Otto and Larry   *Chuck Colson*

August I got wonderful news; Chandra asked Jesus to be her savior and was baptized.

I'd been trying to call Carter for days but couldn't catch him in his office and was frustrated. I'd been in prison eight years and I hoped to have a reduced sentence before I reached ten years. I filled out paperwork for my October board hearing.

September Carter was still trying to schedule a sentence change (from life to 20-40 years), which would give me a minimum of ten years to serve. If he could, according to the parole guidelines, I'd be eligible for parole in a few years.

October Our *Spectator* editor left and Jesse, the activities supervisor, wanted me to take the job. He said I was a steady influence, got along with others and finished what I started. I did not want to be editor or even earn a little more pay. The problems weren't worth it. Jesse decided not to appoint another editor because he knew I'd take on the responsibility, even without the title and pay raise. Getting the *Spectator* out was mainly my doing.

November When I delivered the *Spectator* to Mr. Utess (Jesse's boss), Utess said he didn't worry about a thing as long as I was in control. I hated the responsibility, but was pleased he recognized things were better. The job wasn't as hard as I thought it would be. Besides, working in the *Spectator* office had some advantages. I could type letters to family and friends on the electric typewriter and we always had a coffee pot going. Because the administrators trusted me, I could go almost everywhere in the prison without a pass. I was even allowed to be out of my cell after the 9 p.m. lock-up time. Sometimes I worked on my art in the *Spectator* office.

Carter finally told me that Judge Campbell wouldn't grant me a hearing to reduce my sentence and that the issue of my heavy medication didn't matter to anyone but me. That medication made me so passive that I agreed to anything. It must have affected my understanding and decision-making.

I made $155 when my stepson Kris sold some of my wooden products at his church's bazaar. I asked Kris to use the money to buy Christmas gifts for Mom, Sharon and Sharon's boys.

December Diane and the kids were here to visit me again for Christmas. She got me a new study Bible that made me eager to read and study God's word again. The year had been good and bad, but I felt so blessed by our Lord.

1980

January Diane visited me while Chandra visited Michael next to us. I was so proud of Chandra for making the life of an old man better. Michael loved getting her letters; they really raised his spirits.

February Another stabbing in twelve-block, but the guards just ignored it. A man was stabbed to death on his way to the mess hall. Maybe I should consider a transfer to Northside, the Level 2 security prison next to ours which was smaller and safer. I took the *Spectator* to the print shop there. Sometimes I stayed to help out and the supervisor had offered me a job. Mr. Utess agreed Northside was better and even said he thought I was ready to be released from prison. I enjoyed the challenge of the *Spectator*, but did at least seventy percent of all the work and was tired of it.

Carter told me he'd gone about as far as he could without O'Conner being willing to testify that he was wrong to advise me to accept a life sentence. Carter suggested I get another lawyer but I wasn't sure what to do.

Diane came to visit and I was so focused on seeing her, I forget that Mr. Utess had invited me to eat dinner with him in the officers' dining room. A few days later, he introduced me to a former pastor, Ken Weber, who said he'd heard of me and might be able to help me because he knew attorneys who offered their services for a Jackson half-way house he planned. He promised to contact Carter for more information about my case.

March We had a big baptism ceremony. Eighty of us walked to the Special Activity hall, praising God and singing *"When the Saints Go Marching In!"* Twenty-eight men were baptized in an old bathtub.

A guy who worked in the photo department was stabbed several times. I thought again about a transfer to Northside, even though I'd miss all my friends and even some of the guards at SPSM. First, I'd have to be reclassified to Level 2 security, then recommend a new *Spectator* editor. I could work on my art while waiting.

Carter came with a draft of what he intended to give Judge Campbell, so he hadn't quit yet. Ken still promised his help too. Ken's approach used political pull, which might work because legally I didn't have much hope.

April I talked to Carter on the phone and gave him until June to get me a shorter sentence. He seemed to need a deadline to get anything done.

I hadn't gotten an OK yet to leave the editor's job because Utess hadn't found a replacement he trusted.

An inmate was stabbed in the yard, then came back into the block and hanged himself. The guards left him hanging for several hours, while other inmates walked by and made jokes. No one here valuesd human life. Besides the suicide, three other men were stabbed in one day. Men here fall apart, don't want to face life anymore, so kill themselves gruesomely.

Utess found a new editor, so I quit my job on the *Spectator* to work on some wood projects, which was far more enjoyable. I still did some part-time illustrating and typesetting for the paper, as well as woodworking.

I got a letter from Pastor Settle, and he said he'd write the governor on my behalf. He saw me at my worst and knew the great changes Jesus had made.

Wood-burned picture   Baby cradle

May It was our second wedding anniversary and I was still learning to love Diane the way God's word told me: "Love suffers long and is kind; love does not envy; love does not parade itself, is not puffed up; does not behave rudely, does not seek its own, is not provoked…"

I was active in two Christian fellowship groups because I didn't want to fall back into my old ways of thinking. I was finally able to join a counseling group led by a Christian staff member, too. I was required to complete some counseling or therapy, but wasn't sure if this group would count.

Ken Weber came to see me and we talked a little about my case. Diane had sent him money regularly, most of which probably went to his personal upkeep and not to help my release. I had mixed feelings about him. I hadn't heard anything from Carter either. Was he doing anything?

Gail Light, who worked in MDOC Communications, asked if I would illustrate a booklet to explain prison programs and visiting rules for family members. She wanted simple cartoon-like drawings and couldn't pay me, but she'd ensure I got credit in the booklet. It was fun and I was pleased with the way my drawings turned out.

June Sharon and the boys brought Esther, Chuck's mom, for a visit. I already loved her just from the encouraging letters she'd written me from Florida. She gave me a big hug!

Carter wrote that Judge Campbell's docket was full, so I'd have to wait until July or August for a hearing. He wrote again to say he didn't think Campbell would go along with a sentence reduction. Why have a hearing if it does no good? Ken talked big too, said he's getting people to talk to Judge Campbell, but I doubted if he would.

The officer of our counseling group surprised me when he told us he expected to see me leave prison within a year because I certainly didn't belong in prison any more.

Some of us Christians got together in the evenings for prayer before lockup, but not all were true Christians. To survive in prison, you joined a group for protection, even if you didn't believe the same things as the others. I saw how the fake Christians acted outside of our group.

July Overcrowding and hot weather were a poor mix in the prison; trouble was always brewing. The younger incoming inmates were especially dangerous. We had six stabbings in just one evening and an inmate set the gym on fire, so we were all locked up. Small changes in rules could cause stabbings, fights, and even suicides. There were over twenty knifings this month, often related to drugs. Everyone wanted to control the drug business, which was a big money-maker.

A death contract cost as much as $700. It wasn't safe to sleep unless you locked your cell door. I rigged up a box that jammed my sliding cell door from opening more than a few inches in case someone broke my lock.

August Ken told me his attorney and judge friends want to meet Pastor Settle before they saw Judge Campbell to get a better understanding of my background. Ken had talked with Carter about my case after Carter admitted that his work wasn't going anywhere.

October I went to work in the visiting room taking photos for visitors and inmates. I used the prison's Polaroid camera and inmates and visitors stood against a back wall for photos. When a visit ended, the inmate or his visitor took their photos with them. Just as I snapped one visitor's picture, she pulled her unbuttoned dress wide open and stood there naked. I wasn't sure what to do! If a guard looked at the inmate's photos as he left the visiting room, I could be in big trouble. But if I destroyed the photo, I'd be in bigger trouble with the inmate's friends. I was relieved when the guard didn't check the photos.

I did enjoy the change of routine and most of the guards knew me, so didn't shake me down when I went in and out of the visiting room. Ken was planning some big hoopla on TV featuring my art. Carter still had done nothing.

November While working in the visiting room, a young woman rushed up to the officer's desk. She was hysterical, said her three-week-old baby had stopped breathing. I started praying and saw the baby was turning blue. An officer tried resuscitation until the doctor arrived, but the baby died. I was angry when some of the guards made callous remarks.

Later that day, I heard that an inmate's parents recently died and his wife had just sent him divorce papers so he hung himself. Yes, it was a fine day here.

Seems I already had some pull because of my job in the visiting room. Mom and Dad came to see me while I was working, but Mom forgot to bring her drivers' license, so only Dad was allowed in. I talked to an officer and ten minutes later, Mom walked in and I got a big hug from her.

December It was too late to go back to court for resentencing this year. I was disappointed that neither Carter nor Ken accomplished anything. Diane and the kids came to see me for Christmas. I was so proud to be with my family!

1981

January Diane wrote that she thought we should quit hoping for Ken's help, that he was unreliable and not really a Christian. Yet, he was getting me publicity with his small slide showings of my artwork at churches and to other groups. However, with those shows, he said nothing about the change that Jesus made in my life. He was supposedly a pastor, so why not?

February I got a letter from my old friend Doc. He and his wife had a new daughter. He was working and no longer doing any of the "creative bookkeeping" that had landed him in prison before.

April My friend Larry was released on a special parole and I was happy for him. Before he left, I told him not to conform to society's norm of Christianity, but to the listen to the holy spirit. He had the rest of his life to live as a Christian outside of these walls.

May I met a woman, Barbara Kenyon, on a visit. She was a volunteer with her church's prisoner release center. She was also trying to get my good friend Michael a much-needed eye operation and a medical release. Michael had been living in the infirmary for the past few years because of diabetes and heart problems.

An amusing thing happened in the visiting room when I was taking photos. I saw an inmate quietly slip into the private visitor bathroom. A few minutes later, his girlfriend also went in. Before long—a big crash. The guy slipped quietly back to his seat. About two minutes later, his girlfriend did the same and I guessed what caused the crash. Another woman went in to use the bathroom and came out to report that the sink was down, smashed and there was water on the floor. Later, when the girlfriend left, I saw that the back of her dress was soaked.

The weather got very hot and a riot started, so I kept a detailed journal:

Friday, May 22 I sensed this was coming! For the past four hours we've been locked up. Two blocks are on fire; out my window, I can see black smoke surging out of the officer's dining room and kitchen. To the right, I can see the nurses on the roof of the infirmary with armed guards. No guards are venturing through our block now. One did a while ago—and jars began raining down on him. He was hit several times.

The officer's dining room and kitchen is an inferno. Not just smoke now; the red hot flames are leaping high out the windows. It's part of the auditorium building. If that catches, the whole building will go! The yelling, screaming, laughing and rattling doors are deafening.

The 3- and 4-block inmates are now out on the north yard, surrounded by armed guards. The smoke got so heavy they had to let everyone outside. On TV they have been announcing that all departments of correction guards, regardless of shifts, are to report immediately.

A riot squad of about 30 armed men just went by outside, heading toward the infirmary. All are wearing flak jackets, helmets, walkie-talkies and rifles. A helicopter keeps going around our head. It is so noisy here in the block that I didn't hear the 'copter, but spotted it first. It is really crazy—a carnival. Guys above me are dropping sheets and pillowcases out the windows. A guy outside on the lawn is using them to spell out something on the grass-- for the benefit of the copter no doubt. It says "SEND WOMEN!"

The riot squad is rounding up the loose inmates outside and herding them into the area behind hobbycraft. The officers dining room is still burning. There must be 50 guards now standing by the hobbycraft office. There's the fire department, with about 50 armed guards, standing ready around them.

Late last night two guards were beaten and stabbed. This morning the guards union authorized the prison lockdown. The inmates who weren't locked down yet took over 3-block and 4-block, the commissary, paint shop and officer's dining room and began setting them all on fire. So far only one inmate has been stabbed.

There's two fire trucks outside now and they seem to have the officers dining room under control. There's still a huge cloud coming from the north. The riot squad is standing at ready, facing 11-block with guns up. According to TV, the blue and white copter overhead is flying with Perry Johnson, head of the Department of Corrections.

We've been locked up seven hours now. The fires are all out and it's relatively quiet. The riot squad came in with cold sandwiches for us and that set things off again! Half the men in the block threw their sandwiches off the upper galleys, so now not only is there glass, paper, clothes and rags on the base floor, but also bologna and bread. I hadn't eaten anything since lunchtime yesterday so the sandwich tastes good to me! I wolfed it down.

I hear that on the north yard there are still 200 to 300 inmates refusing to return to their blocks. The state police are surrounding the north side yard. TV reports that five inmates have been beaten or stabbed and taken to the hospital. Warden Mintzes announced over the PA system that he is concerned about the inmates in the yard. He thanks them in advance for getting to their cells in an orderly way saying the administration is not interested in punishing anyone.

Getting dark. They're crazy here in 11-block again. Two guards just came through and inmates threw glass jars at them. It's dangerous for any guard, and not the safest for us living on the base floor either. Glass chunks come in under the door and one chunk even landed on my bed. It's too dangerous now for guards to come through with food for us.

Saturday, May 23 I had no sleep at all. My eyes are red and burning from the smoke of little fires set on the base floor all night. It's still a madhouse. The guards tried to bring something for us to eat, but these fools rained down jars to stop them. Are these fools thinking, "We'll get even with them -- we'll refuse to eat!"? Dumb! I ate my breakfast and thanked God for it.

Still rattling and banging on the doors. It's deafening! I was wood-burning a breadboard and one of the visiting room guards (who knows me) stood watching. He told me to bring over my wood for him to see. He took it for a minute, then handed it back and said "take what's in my left hand." I did-and he'd given me $11 worth of the tokens we used in place of money! He found them while assessing the resident store damage, and wanted me to have them.

Sunday, May 24 Things are a little quieter. We heard that at the beginning of this riot, two men tried (unsuccessfully) to get keys away from a guard. I heard that a group had plotted to take over the infirmary, killing until their demands were

met. I didn't realize how much splintered
glass had flown into my cell until I shook
out my blanket.

As soon as the visiting room opened
today, Kris, Chuck, Sharon and their boys
came to visit me and to make sure I was OK.
It was so good to see them! I ask them to
call Diane and Chandra, to let them know
I'm all right.

The warden–trying to be decent–lets
everyone spend some time outside and take
showers. What do these fools do? Some break
into the inmate store's storeroom to loot
everything they can carry off. My block–the
"honor block"-turns into a rushing,
clamoring circus. Guys stream back carrying
cases of cigarettes, cosmetics, canned
foods, everything! Officials attempt to
stop the looting but then give up. Another
fire or two is set in the vocational
building. Again, party time all night.

Monday, May 25 We're allowed to go to the
mess hall. Then it takes two hours to get
some of the fools here to lock back up
after the meal. We're supposed to go
outside for yard time if nothing else
happens. Last time, they looted the
storeroom. I'm going to try and get some
rest while everyone else is outside and
it's quiet. As evening comes, we are still
locked up and the inmates are beginning to
raise the roof again.

Tuesday, May 26 We were off to a normal
routine at 6:30 a.m. By noon, guys were
breaking in every place they could. At
Northside the residents set every one of
the modular buildings on fire, plus the
blocks they share with us in Central. They
almost completely destroyed all their
living areas.

The warden has bent over backwards to
keep things calm. Every time he tries to
let us out of lockup, fools cause havoc.
We're still locked up for most of the day.

On the radio, a reporter standing over 100 yards away from the Northside block fires says he feels the heat at that distance. Many fire departments are here; and ambulances and state troopers are all around the Northside complex. Some inmates are trapped. I have no idea where the MDOC will house the 1,000 men at the Northside complex; their kitchen, dining room, academic and vocational buildings are destroyed too.

I managed to get to the store to buy a loaf of bread, a jar of peanut butter, and two cans of chili. Not a banquet, but better than nothing. I wish Warden Mintzes would stop coddling these fools and just keep us in lockdown for a good while. I think, "If it comes down to it, I'm ready, praise Jesus!" A wonderful feeling, no fear of dying.

I don't see the huge columns of smoke from Northside anymore; the fire must be under control. It's quieted down in the block except for an occasional fool yelling.

At suppertime, the kitchen crew came into the block with carts of food. They set it out on one of the center tables to pass out, but the stupid fools upstairs went wild, throwing cigarettes, jars and toilet paper down into the food. Insanity.

All day, inmates are angry with the guards and administrators. Now they turn on each other: verbal fights, threats, name-calling, and challenges to other inmates. These screwballs have lost all sense of reality. It finally quiets down about midnight.

Wednesday May 27 We are still locked down tight; I hope they keep it this way. There is no Northside any more, it was completely destroyed. There's still no definite number of how many people were overcome by smoke or injured.

What bothers me most is no mail! I feel very cut off. At noon, I spotted guards sorting the mail and think, thank You, Jesus! I try to do some woodworking, but it's hard to concentrate. I have to keep an eye out for burning toilet paper that may float into my cell. I get a short nap and wake up to hear the warden saying that the guards and personnel are worn out, so an indefinite lockdown is necessary. He apologized to those who are not responsible for this mess. In the evening, thank you, Jesus, I got two wonderful letters!

Know what kicked this all off? Aside from overcrowding and loss of incentives, the union planned that the guards would lock everyone up last Friday and walk off the job. That was a stupid move-to lock us up over a holiday weekend! We'd miss our holiday dinner, movie and extra time in the yard. These may sound like small things, but in here they're very important.

What is so stupid is that the inmates think they have the upper hand. In the midst of all this, I just thank Jesus for the love I have in my life, knowing my friends and family are praying for me. In all this, I actually have peace. And one bright spot, mail is now coming in.

Saturday, May 30 We are still in lock-up. Things are a bit quieter, so I can actually get a good night's sleep. Except for not having a shower, I don't mind the lock-up. Gives me time to read, write letters and do some artwork. We have TV too. Today I saw on the news that some inmates decided to go on a hunger strike. Really smart, huh? I heard that the guards had permission to keep us locked up for their own safety. This may sound crazy, but I'm on the guards' side.

June, three weeks later We were still locked up and the

99

guards threatened a strike. I heard through the prison grapevine that there were plans to divide up the huge central complex and erect eight-foot fences, topped with barbed wire between the sections. I thought it was a good idea! We remained in lockup until the fenced divisions were done. We also had another major shakedown because the guards were sure there were still hidden weapons.

July 1 We were only on nighttime lockup when a 29-year-old was found dead from a heart attack early one morning. The guards were supposed to make night rounds, but apparently didn't. We had occasional showers. I was able to call Diane so she knew I was OK. There were rumors that the guards were threatening a strike that would mean complete lockup over the Fourth of July holiday.

Later in July Lockup was finally over and I went back to work as photographer in the visiting room. I heard on the news that a crowd of people had marched from downtown Jackson to the prison to demand a halt to our lockdown.

Diane typed my account of the riot and sent copies to Ken and Carter. She also sent copies to Judge Campbell, the parole board and one to me. The prison refused to give me my copy and returned it to Diane. I laughed that it must have been too inflammable for me, the author, to read!

I heard that a new facility was opening in Ypsilanti and a few trustworthy workers were needed for key jobs to assist the staff, so Mr. Utess put my name on the screening list. Our living conditions there would be much better.

Ken Weber came to see me, all excited. He said his program was exploding, which was good for him and me. At the last showing of my art in Lansing, MDOC personnel came, as well as reporters. He said I'm on the way toward a release. Coming from Ken, I had doubts.

August It didn't sound good for any of us who had hoped to work at Ypsilanti. I stopped asking.

Ken set up an art show in Rose City featuring some of my art and was taping a TV interview for it. Several officers told me they hoped he would push, so I could go home soon. One invited me to join him for lunch in the officers' dining room. I had a good time as we talked about our families. Another officer told me he thinks my time at SPSM was coming to an end. Maybe there was hope?

My good friend Michael didn't get his medical release; instead he died peacefully while sitting in a wheelchair in his room. The Porters contacted one of his relatives to handle his burial. I was glad Michael was not buried in the inmate potter's field, Cherry Hill. The photos I'd seen of it were dismal–small insignificant wooden markers with dates and an inmate number, the field overgrown and not taken care of. Michael's in heaven. When Doc left, then Michael, big parts of me left too.

Barbara, who had helped Michael, visited me a few times. I introduced her to Bruce, a Christian friend at SPSM. They hit it off right away and I wondered if there might be budding romance between them.

September Jesse asked me again to come back to work as *Spectator* editor. I considered it because it might help efforts toward my early release.

Because of all the unrest, we still lived in a sort of concentration camp. We were on half rations, the prison split up with concertina that divided the sections, even though the coiled barbed wire was against the law to use inside a prison. We got tickets if we even spit! Tension was still very high for both inmates and staff; serious beatings and stabbings happened every few days.

October Three of us moved all the *Spectator* stuff back to the office; it was hard physical work. The entire office had been searched by guards and torn apart during the riot. We had to re-order all the supplies and some equipment before we could do anything again. Maybe I should put in for full-time hobbycraft work instead.

I heard that about a third of the inmates at SPSM had

tuberculosis, so everyone got a TB skin test. The plumbing in the building is about eighty years old and constantly leaked sewage, so I wasn't surprised.

A fellow was stabbed with a butcher knife while working in the kitchen; he was just a kid and dead by the time a guard got to him.

November In spite of my misgivings, I officially accepted the job as *Spectator* editor again.

Carter came to see me and surprisingly, it was an uplifting visit. He said he was truly sorry he was unable to help me and I believed him. He did all he could. I wrote a letter to the court to officially dismiss him. His office had been handling my case for over seven years with absolutely no results.

1982

January I wrote Carter to ask him to send me all the legal documents in my case because Ken needed them. I believed what Ken told us was 15-20 percent truthful and 80-85 percent things he would like to see happen.

February A reporter from the *Jackson Citizen Patriot* wanted to do a feature article on someone who had an interesting pastime or hobby. Mr. Utess gave him my name. The journalist, Brian, was easy to talk to but knew very little about art and I had to explain the differences in various mediums. He asked about my faith and family, my favorite subjects. His article turned out to be a full-page spread.

Past haunts future of model prisoner, gifted artist

Christianity, marriage may aid parole chances.
By BRIAN DEMING

Jackson Citizen Patriot staff writer

Robert Otto Bryan cut the throats of two people he never knew and let them die as their 3-year-old and 18-month-old children watched.

102

Fannie Freudenburg, matron of the Cass County jail, remembers the murders that shook the Cassopolis area 10 years ago. She also remembers the man held in jail for killing Timothy and Arlene Roderick.

"He is sort of a quiet fellow, sort of a loner," said Mrs. Freudenburg. "I remember that he did a lot of sketching. Most of it is pictures of things that were dead."

Robert Otto Bryan, now 43, still sketches. He draws in his cell in Block 11 at Southern Michigan Prison. This murderer, a slender man with a goatee and mournful eyes, is a model prisoner and an artist. People who know him feel he doesn't belong in prison. People who know his work believe he has talent that will some day be critically recognized.

"I ended up killing two people I didn't know and wouldn't know if they were sitting where you are," Bryan told a reporter in the office of The Spectator, the prison newspaper that Bryan edits. "Then what do you do after something like that?"

What Bryan did, after about a year in prison, is to dedicate himself to art.

"I bought a set of colored inks and a bottle of polymer and made paints out of it," said Bryan. One of his first paintings while in prison was "Boyhood Memories." He sold it for $75.

"I got into it as a way of doing something," said Bryan. "I didn't do it for gain. But, you know, it's the best thing I ever did."

Working alone in his cell, Bryan has worked with opaque water colors; inks, tempera, oils, acrylics. He has done assemblage pieces–compositions made from scraps of junk and odds and ends. He has done block carving and woodwork. He has done sculpture.

He has bought his own materials. Some materials, such as modeling clay, are not allowed in prison. So Bryan made his own with materials he had available.

Some pieces he has sold on the outside for as much as $400. One piece–"Cell Assemblage," a representation off a cell wall– hangs in a state office building in Detroit. His work has been shown in exhibits, in galleries and malls throughout southern Michigan.

He has gained neither great wealth nor critical acclaim. But, with his talent, he has earned thousands of dollars. Much of that money he has given away. He has given money to Youth Haven, for example, a camp near Rives Junction for underprivileged children.

And, while he is not widely known, his work has been recognized.

"Technically, he is one of the best," said Thomas Rudd, a free-lance sculptor from Tecumseh who became familiar with Bryan's work when he was an art instructor in a program that has since been discontinued.

Rudd feels that Bryan has to develop more as an artist.

"Esthetically, probably some college training would do him a world of good," said Rudd.

But Rudd is convinced the talent is there.

Rudd remembers the last time he saw Bryan. He told Bryan he expected to see his work someday in a New York gallery. "Personally, I think he'll make it," said Rudd.

Actually, Bryan gained modest recognition for his art before entering Southern Michigan Prison. One painting, "The Invitation," which Bryan did when he lived in Missouri, hangs in the foyer of the Concordia Publishing House in St. Louis. The painting is Bryan's image of Christ beckoning guests to the Last Supper.

Perhaps prophetically, that painting with the highly religious theme was done before Bryan experienced his own religious rebirth.

Bryan said he became a Christian after a year in prison. Bryan credits his faith as being a source of strength for him. It also has been a theme in much of Bryan's work.

Bryan said he is particularly proud of his series of paintings titled "Man Without God," a surreal image of hollow, featureless, human-like figures on a desolate plane.

Behind the walls of prison, caged among society's outcasts, Bryan has found more than he believes he could have found in society, more than seems possible in prison.

Prison, Bryan said, gave him stability that he never knew. As a child, he never finished one full year of school in the same place until he was a freshman in high school. His home life was always in flux. His mother married six times. His first marriage did not give him stability, he said. "That was a bad marriage from the beginning," he said.

Incredibly, since becoming an inmate, Bryan has found a family, and, he said he enjoys a happier family life than he ever knew.

Actually, the family found Bryan.

Diane Russell, an art instructor, visited an exhibit of Bryan's paintings at Adrian. She was so impressed she wrote to Bryan and eventually visited him.

They used to talk about how ridiculous marriage in prison is, said Bryan.

But in 1978, they married.

And along with a wife, he has new in-laws and two step-children. And, they have made him feel he really belongs, he says, a feeling he has never known before.

"I've got it better today than I ever have in my life," said Bryan. "It took 39 years to have a real mom and dad." Mrs. Bryan now works for IBM at Poughkeepsie, N.Y. Bryan hopes to go there when he is released from prison. His dream is to set up a studio of his own.

For all that he has found in prison, prison has not given him the freedom he feels he needs as an artist. Many materials and tools are not available to him, and, of course, he has no opportunity to see the world outside the prison.

"I've had a lifelong curse of being creative," said Bryan. "Needless to say, in a place like this it's really restricted."

Indeed, Bryan has become so frustrated with the limitations imposed by the prison that he hasn't worked on a serious art project in two years, although he continues to sketch to keep his eye and hand in practice.

Bryan will soon be within reach of that freedom he craves. In May, he will have completed the minimum 10 years of his 10-years-to-life sentence for second-degree murder. He is already eligible for a parole board hearing.

To prison staff members, there could hardly be anyone more deserving of a hearing. Administrators, in fact, have been so impressed with Bryan that they sought him out to be editor of The Spectator when it was recently re-issued, a position he held before but was not seeking.

"I have found him to be honest and sincere," said Mr. Utess, director of resident services at the prison. He said that Bryan's coming to grips with his God and religion, his good marriage and his dedication to art, contribute to his positive attitude.

"I think he's ready," said Mr. Utess. "He's as ready as he ever will be."

The Rev. Ken Weber, who manages the Challenge Project at 109 W. Franklin, agrees. The Challenge Project is a program that has helped inmates and former inmates.

"He is completely rehabilitated," said Weber. "I think he has done this himself, with very little help from the prison system."

While Bryan may have satisfied prison officials and friends on the outside, he may not have satisfied society and the parole board.

The April 1972 murders of the Rodericks in their farmhouse near Cassopolis stunned the rural south-western Michigan community.

"The people were scared," said Howard D. Sheline of Marcellus, then a sergeant in the Cass County Sheriff's Department and the first officer at the scene.

Bryan was caught in Florida less than a month after the murders. He was charged with two counts of first-degree murder and one count of manslaughter, the manslaughter for the death of an unborn child. Mrs. Roderick was within days of delivering the family's third child. Bryan was never tried. A plea bargain produced a guilty plea for one count of second-degree murder. Weber believes any hint of Bryan's release is not likely to sit well with people in Cass County.

Certainly a strike against Bryan are recent stories about model inmates or talented inmates who fail outside of prison. Particularly ominous is the highly publicized example of Jack Henry Abbott, an author of a book of letters from prison and a literary protégé of Pulitzer Prize-winning author Norman Mailer.

Just six weeks after being released from prison, Abbott killed a man.

A more recent example is that of Pete Grenier, a model prisoner at SMP who is supposedly gifted and is back in police custody for allegedly attempting to abduct a woman near Charlotte only days after being placed on parole.

"I flinch every time I see those things,"' said Bryan. "It really hurts because you know you are not like that. I've had 10 years of introspection. I've grown in here."

Bryan explains his crime as a sort of breakdown. "I felt boxed in a corner with no way out," Bryan said. "I just lost it."

He had been a plant superintendent for a company in Missouri. The company got into financial trouble, first cut his salary and then cut his job. Meanwhile, his wife underwent three cancer operations. Bryan couldn't get a job and creditors hounded him.

"I saw it all go, a piece at a time," Bryan said. Finally, Bryan just took off in his car. He found himself on the highway "obsessed by fours." He saw everything in sets of fours. He would stop the car and look at a sign or something by the road and look for letters or words or objects in fours. He would become angry if he didn't recognize four items, if there were only three-of-a-kind or two-of-a-kind.

His car broke down. He went to the nearest farmhouse. No one was home. He went in to look for something to repair the car. When the Rodericks returned, he hid in the closet. In the closet was a shotgun. With it, Bryan forced the couple to lie down. Bryan tied them up and killed them.

"My first reaction was, 'Do I really want to maintain this relationship'?" said Mrs. Bryan who was uneasy at first when she learned about why her husband-to-be is in prison. "I finally came to the conclusion that he really has changed."

"I have no concerns," said Mrs. Bryan, "I've seen him mature a lot. I really don't think he'll ever get into trouble with the law. I think I can watch out and make sure he has the freedom to go ahead and create."

April Ken was making my name recognized by my art shows, but the public climate in Michigan was not good and no one trusted inmates. We had more stabbings here and an inmate apparently fell from the third floor gallery in five block. Things were restless enough that we were in lockup again. It wasn't as bad as the riot, but we were all tense.

June Typical month here: A good man, Jack, had a heart attack. Nearby inmates saw him and yelled for the guard. It took fifteen minutes for a guard to meander to Jack's cell, another fifteen until a nurse came from the infirmary, although it was right next to our block. Jack had stopped breathing by then. The nurse went back to the infirmary.

After twenty minutes, the doctor came.

I'd missed another stabbing party, right in front of my cell. I saw the attackers taken to the hole, with two men who were stabbed still on the floor, waiting for medics.

The other side of SPSM had a minor riot. We heard gun shots and the deputy on the bullhorn asked everyone to return to their units, so we had another long lockdown to look forward to. At least I was well stocked with supplies: Bible tapes, radio, my Bible, paper and stamps, art supplies, canned food and peanut butter–and even five packs of gum. What more could a guy want? The sirens were blowing, doors rattling, things thrown out of the cells, crashing to the main floor below. The deputy was still trying to get everyone into their housing units.

October I was moved to a different cell again, so once more I had to get rid of the roaches the last man left behind. I didn't know how guys could live in a filthy cell. I sprayed with heavy duty stuff, soaked from top to bottom, then watched as the roaches scrambled to leave. Once they were gone, I used a bucket of disinfectant and wiped down all the walls and floor. When it was all dry, I moved in and got settled.

Ken had been involved for over two years and Diane had sent him money regularly, yet every major thing he'd promised to do for me was still undone. The slide shows of my artwork benefitted his Challenge Program far more than they did me. I once thought of Ken as a helpful friend; but no longer trusted what he said.

Northside was rebuilt as well as it could be.

1983

January No word from Ken about his scheduled meeting with my judge; he was even slower than Carter was.

February Ken surprised me! He said he'd met Judge Campbell, the meeting went well, and he planned to set up a slide show of my art in the State capital building. He also gave me a copy of a letter to the parole board from my prosecutor and said not to let them know I had it.

October 5, 1982
Corrections Commission, Parole Board
C/o Mr. Edward S. Turner, Chairperson
Re: Parole for Robert Otto Bryan
    Dear Mr. Turner,
    I am writing on behalf of the Cass County Prosecutor's Office with respect to the possibility of parole for inmate Robert Otto Bryan. As you are probably aware, Mr. Bryan was convicted back in the early seventies for second degree murder here in Cass County.

    There has been some recent publicity concerning the possibility of parole for Mr. Bryan since he has served the minimum ten (10) year requirement to be considered for parole. I am in my second term as prosecutor and previous to that time served as chief assistant prosecutor, assistant prosecutor and legal intern in the Cass County office. I am familiar with the details of the case since I handled some of the appellate work on the case. The case was actually prosecuted by my former boss and now Circuit Judge, the Honorable Michael E. Dodge.

    I would hope that as a prosecutor for the past eight years here in Cass County I would have a firm grasp of the community feeling toward Mr. Bryan being granted parole by your board, but my remarks are mine and mine alone.

    I have read with interest the accomplishments that Mr. Bryan has made over the years while an inmate at Jackson and find them laudable. I also feel that our system of justice must as some time reward those who have been punished for their crimes and make a sincere effort to "rehabilitate" themselves. However, I must balance those feelings with the sense that our system must extract a fair penalty for those convicted of crimes, especially one as heinous as in this case.

The senseless slaughter of a young couple along with an expectant child was perhaps the worst, if not one of the worst crimes this county has seen in modern times. I feel compelled to urge you not to release Mr. Bryan at this time because in my opinion the criminal justice system has not yet extracted a sufficient punishment for the crime inflicted on those innocent victims.

I would urge every member of the parole board to search his/her own conscience in deliberating on this case, mindful of the terrible waste of human life and potential inflicted by Mr. Bryan.

The criminal justice system to be respected must appear to all to be fair in its handling of both the offender and the victim, ten (10) years cannot in my opinion be deemed sufficient punishment for a crime of this nature. I request that Mr. Bryan's parole be denied at this time.

Sincerely,
William T. Grimmer
Prosecuting Attorney

Our counselor asked me to fill out a parole evaluation report (PER); that usually meant a change was coming. I hoped to receive a lower custody rating so I could transfer to Northside. I was more than ready to leave SPSM! Mr. Utess told me, "Northside next week, Otto!" I packed, glad I wouldn't die in SPSM. I wrote Diane to tell her that when I did die, to have a small funeral with a party afterwards; to drink wine and pray I squeaked through heaven's gates.

March The call came and I was ready to go! Goodbye SPSM, my home for the past nine years, and hello Northside. I hoped I would never be back at SPSM.

Jackson (Northside)

March, 1983

Northside was quieter and cleaner, and I didn't have to scrub or even sweep my new cell before I unpacked. It was nearly bare; just a bunk, desk and chair–no locker or shelf to store my clothes or belongings. Until I had a formal work assignment, I'd be locked in here most of the time. The rules were strict but I was OK with that. As I came back from breakfast the day after I arrived, I spied an empty cell with a locker, so zipped in, grabbed the locker and dragged it to my cell. I washed it out and hung up my clothes.

We couldn't hang anything on the walls, like I had in my cell studio at SPSM, so I just put a calendar and a few family photos on the bulletin board over my desk.

One day at lunch a guy at my table asked if my wedding ring was real gold. I told him yes. He challenged, "You can get that taken off of you." I calmly said "You can try." End of that! (My experiences at Woodburn paid off.)

Visiting was better than at SPSM too, quieter and less crowded, and we were allowed seven visits a month, not five. The guards also allowed couples to do more cuddling. I learned the guys here called SPSM "Central" because, although we were attached to it, we were actually a different prison and lower security level.

One day I had two visits and three job offers. The first visitor was Ken, who again promised he'd promote me (with his phony politics and strategy). I'd told Ken more than once to talk about the way Jesus changed my life when he showed my art, instead of simply saying that I had a "religious

111

experience," but I didn't think he did it. I once considered him a helpful friend, but no longer. Mom and Dad were my other visitors and I loved seeing them. My job offers were at the woodshop (hobbycraft), as a block worker and in the print shop. The print shop offer was my best option.

Evelyne Porter came to see me too. While waiting for her, I chatted with the guard, told him I'd been in honor block and my last job assignment was visiting room photographer. As I left my visit, he didn't even strip search me.

April I got my hobbycraft card (needed to order and keep craft tools and other art materials in my cell) and spent the morning in the wood hobbycraft shop. I hoped to work there one morning a week, help the woodworkers and do some paperwork, and I could also use the power tools for my own projects.

My friends Bruce and Barbara were engaged and I was happy for them.

I started work at the print shop. A dozen men worked there, plus our supervisor Roy. We printed jobs for all the Michigan prisons, not just Northside.

I heard some college business courses were offered at Northside, and I decided to take some to be ready to run my own business when I got home.

A visiting room guard told me that all the honor status in Central was gone. The government did away with good time, which also had encouraged better behavior. Most jobs were gone too, so inmates got money from friends and relatives, or stole from each other. There were few incentives to encourage men to leave prison better than when they came in. I prayed that God would get me home soon.

I learned the printing job quickly and really enjoyed running the presses. It felt good to do physical work again. When Sharon visited, she teased me about my inky fingernails.

May Our fifth wedding anniversary was coming up, but

Diane couldn't come until the end of the month. I hoped to be home for our sixth one. I was forty-six and had almost eleven years in, counting the time in the jail and Forensic Center. My next parole hearing was July of next year. I was working at the print shop and woodworking in my spare time, making owl and bellow-shaped clocks.

I learned how to unjam an ink roller, three times in one day! The other guys kidded me so I told them I was now an expert at press cleaning. I was paid 90¢ a day; the top daily pay in the print shop was $1.36. I made more money selling my wood products, even with the twenty percent that the prison gift shop got for selling them.

June Because of the overcrowding, the board wanted all lifer records brought up to date for possible release after ten years. ('Lifers' were men and women with second degree life sentences like mine.) It probably wouldn't help me because the prosecutor and sheriff in Cassopolis still objected to my release, so I'd have to wait.

Hobbycraft card   Bellow and owl clocks   Banjo clocks

July I made $39.62 for the month of June at the print shop. My clocks were selling well too. Some of the staff ordered them early for Christmas gifts. I made clocks for Diane and Chandra shaped like banjos.

August I sold a clock for $60 and spent most of the money on more materials to make more clocks to sell.

Ken asked me to write a rebuttal of what Dr. Tanay wrote about me in his book because some of it was false. He thought perhaps the board had the copy of Tanay's story in my file. Ken had broken so many promises of meetings on my behalf that I didn't trust what he said. But who else would keep my name and case alive? I needed someone *like* him, but *not* him! He wasn't working for free, either–Diane still sent him monthly checks.

October Diane agreed with my feelings about Ken so we decided he'd get no more checks except for reimbursement (with proof for something he'd already done for me). He probably was just a con man. I still had hope that Judge Campbell would reduce my sentence as he got nearer retirement age.

November Only two of us were running the five printing presses; I got off work very tired. Most of the other men had transferred to the chair factory at Northside (which paid better). After new guys were hired, I trained them on the presses and looked forward to a Thanksgiving break. Not only was I thankful for my family and a day off work, we also had a good holiday meal with all the trimmings.

At the end of the month Sharon came alone for a visit. She said they may go to Florida for Christmas to visit Chuck's parents.

December It started snowing all night, was only 20 degrees out. The snow got so deep the supervisors couldn't get in to work, so we had a day off work. I finished some woodworking projects for Christmas, and all I could think of was that Diane was coming.

I watched a program about the future of personal computers on TV, and it fired me up to learn more about them. Saving energy was also in the news. I visualized Diane and me living in an earth-bermed solar-heated house, so did a sketch of my dream house. Diane could write manuals with a computer remotely connected to IBM's mainframe, and I'd have a workshop with a computer to keep track of my materials, orders and shipping.

Christmas Day I had a wonderful visit with Diane, Mom and Dad. Our Lord had so blessed me. Being with them always made me feel I belonged and at peace, full of hope and confidence.

1984

January I hated to see Diane leave Michigan, especially because it was snowing and she had a seven hundred mile trip back. She promised to come in February again.

Guards took five guys to the hole because someone was stabbed. It was only the second stabbing since I'd been at Northside, quite a change from Central.

March The Northside chaplain wanted a platform with wheels to move the chapel organ around, so called me to his office to discuss what he'd need. We talked, but not only about the platform. He asked about my family, plans and future. He prayed with me and I left feeling good, touched by his words and the music of the prison choir practicing in the background.

I was finally in group therapy, run by a prison psychologist, Dr. Klass. 'Official' therapy was required before I could be considered for release. I wasn't sure how helpful it would be but went to every session anyway.

April It was not looking good for getting more hobbycraft shop space or equipment at Northside. I heard that space was at a premium so the woodshop might have to close completely down.

May Diane was here for our anniversary. I made her one of my wood design projects, a donkey stand for a small plant. I learned my scheduled parole hearing for July would be delayed.

The hobbycraft shop found space to expand and had a new supervisor, Char. I told Roy I'd like to transfer to hobbycraft and he wasn't surprised. He said he expected it because my back got quite sore standing and running the presses. It was all right with him, but he said he'd miss me.

June Frederick and Lois Danker came to see me. I loved them and hoped Diane could meet them one day. They were my first real family outside of my grandparents, Otto and Nellie.

I talked to Chuck on the phone and he told me that Dad had a malignant tumor in his chest. I called and talked to Dad; he was upbeat and would have surgery soon. When Diane got back to Michigan, she and Mom came to visit and told me that Dad had surgery, most of his cancer was removed and he was doing well. At the end of the month, Mom and Dad stopped on the way back from his first radiation treatment. He looked good and was in good spirits.

August I heard through the grapevine that I wouldn't have a parole hearing at all this year. Diane wrote that I should stand up more for myself and not always depend on others to do it for me. Thinking about my crime made me feel my guilt and shame again, so put me in a bad mood. I knew Diane was right about standing up for who I was now, so I wrote letters to Judge Campbell, Senator Vaughn, and the board chairman. Senator Vaughn answered my letter and said he'd do what he could to help with a parole.

The hobbycraft shop was shut down because nearby groups complained about our dust and machine noise. I couldn't make any more things to sell.

The corrections ombudsman came to see me after I wrote him and questioned why the board skipped my last review. He set up a meeting with the head of the board, Diane and Senator Vaughn.

September After the meeting with the board chairman,

Senator Vaughn sent a letter to the board stating he was in favor of my parole.

Because the hobbycraft shop was closed, I went back to work in the print shop. I didn't stop woodworking but without power tools, switched to hand-sculpted wood cattails that I could make in my cell after work. They each had a dragonfly and a small bird's nest with wooden eggs and sold quite well in the hobbycraft store. I made Mom and Diane each one.

October I was called for a surprise parole board hearing and the board member seemed as surprised as I was. I didn't see Campbell's or Vaughn's recommendation letters in my file but the prosecutor's letter against my parole was right on top and she talked mostly about that. I asked her why the negative things were always discussed, rather than the positive but she didn't answer.

Diane got the new "toy" she'd been wanting–her first personal computer, an IBM PC Junior. She wrote me long computer-generated letters, with all the characters formed by dots. She also picked out a newborn miniature Schnauzer. I wasn't sure which she'd enjoy more, the computer or the puppy.

We had a bad day. It was the last game of the World Series and our electricity was off because the administrators decided to update some wiring. Inmates were irate, and I was surprised they didn't start a riot.

I worked half days in the print shop, with the rest of my time spent making clocks, Bible stands, cattail and toadstool sculptures for the prison store. Some of the staff gave me orders for Christmas gifts.

November Mom and Dad came to see me; Dad was still feeling good and done with his radiation treatments.

We had a nice Thanksgiving dinner here: turkey legs, cranberries and dressing, sweet potatoes, salad and pumpkin pie. After we ate, I planned to watch the football game but was so full I fell asleep on my bunk instead.

December I signed up to take three college courses starting in January, taught here by local instructors.

Diane and her new puppy were in Michigan for Christmas. I wished she could bring the pup in to meet me. I remembered my dog Pepper and still loved dogs; Kay and I had a teacup poodle that I enjoyed playing with. I made dog beds for Diane's puppy and Kris' little Schnauzer.

Toadstools   *Bible stands*   *Dog beds*

1985

January I felt horrible, so saw the doctor who said I had flu and perhaps an infected kidney. I'd just started college classes but skipped them for a week, even though the antibiotic helped some. No sense infecting anyone else.

February Mid-term time; so far, I had a B average. Steve came back as supervisor of the hobbycraft shop and offered me a job as a clerk. He let me use the power tools for my own projects.

April Classes were over. I enjoyed them but was glad to have time for more woodworking.

I signed up for an UpJohn medical trial to test whether a new medicine might grow hair on balding men. The testing lasted for four months and I'd earn $360–more than I made working for a whole year.

May Our anniversary came, but not Diane. She had visited in April, and it was too soon for her to make another long trip. I started new classes in business psychology and

118

small business management. I knew I'd do well when I left here after I got my first perfect exam score in class.

Chandra drove by herself to Michigan to visit family and came to see me. I enjoyed every minute with her.

June We were on a precautionary standby because of a small riot going on in Central, six guards injured, one seriously hurt. All our work assignments were cancelled and more guards roamed around. It took three days to get back to normal. Then, another small uprising inside Central a few days later; eight guards and one inmate were hurt and a female guard had her jaw broken.

In unrelated news, a doctor for the Upjohn trial found one big hair on my test patch.

July I woke up to the hollering, incoherent gibberish of an inmate mental case. About twice a week he went crazy and should have been in a mental hospital, not in prison. When he started yelling, the other men yelled back at him to shut up and that got him going all the more. I wished they'd all be quiet.

August My skin tests were finished and I didn't grow any more hair that I could see.

Our unit counselor asked if I'd like to transfer to Kinross, in the Upper Peninsula. I said "No way–it's too far from my family." Our food improved when we got civilian cooks in the kitchen. Inmates still helped but our potatoes were now cooked, not half raw and the chili was the best I'd tasted since I got here.

My cattail pieces were selling well in the hobbycraft store. One day, spread out on my cot were four cart planters, two bellow clocks, one owl bellow, twelve plaques and one cattail-with-dragonfly piece.

Prison wasn't always serious and dull. I joked with two female guards in our visiting room:

I said to the new guard: "Don't let that guard, Cathy, mislead you; she's ornery as the dickens."

New guard to Cathy: "This fellow tells me not to let you mislead me."

Cathy looked at me: "Oh, that trouble maker?" Then she turned to me: "Aren't I always nice to your wife?"

I replied: "Well, yes. Much nicer than I am most of the time."

New guard to me, very seriously: "Aren't you nice to your wife? You could change, you know."

Cathy and I started laughing, and the new guard realized we were just kidding. Cathy then told her how nice Diane was and that she worked for IBM.

September I started algebra and data processing classes. The computer instructor talked ninety miles a minute, tossed out acronyms like COBOL, RPG, JCL, and FORTRAN. I told Diane that he thought IBM was the god of the industry. I got 90 percent on my first algebra test but it was the highest grade I got the rest of the semester. Algebra proved to be drudgery for me; business math is what I really needed. I felt pressured with two classes, wishing I had more time for woodworking; that's what brought in money.

October I decided to sell my dog leash hangers through a magazine ad and Diane helped me write a business plan. She had a professional photographer take a photo of a leash hanger to run in *Dog Fancy* magazine, under the business name "Wood 'n Things." I designed order forms and envelopes and had dog frames stacked up, ready to add the dogs' names as orders came in. Bob Porter said he'd add the names and then ship them for me.

I was still making doll cradles, owl clocks, swing planters, plaques and cattails for Christmas sales at the hobbycraft store.

Clock   *Another dog leash hanger*   *Doll cradle*

I heard on the news that at Central, an inmate died of AIDS and that there were three more cases. One was an inmate who just transferred to Northside. As soon as he was diagnosed, six other inmates here begged to be tested (after previously denying any close involvement with the man).

I had trouble writing a BASIC program and we didn't have a computer to test it, so I decided to drop the data processing class; it took too much of my time. I was still going to group therapy with Dr. Klass, taking the business class and getting wood pieces ready to sell as Christmas gifts.

November A lieutenant offered me the job of visiting room photographer at Northside, but the offer came too late. I was too busy with woodworking and classes. Also, the woodworkers at Central asked for help to make Christmas toys, so I was part of a "Santa workshop," turning out toys for children in Jackson-area communities. We went into Central every day to make puzzles, rocking horses, doll cradles, kiddie stools, toy cars, trucks, tanks, trains and simple puzzles. It was a good feeling, bringing joy to children who had little, but left me less time to earn money for my family's Christmas gifts. I did manage to make some string toys to sell.

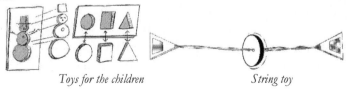

Toys for the children   *String toy*

I also had to get my Wood 'n Things ad into *Dog Fancy* by early December for the March issue, so I worked to finish that too. Jesse helped me make two doll cradles and they sold right away; I wish we had time to make more!

We had our second AIDS death here. Mom and Dad came to visit me too. It was a hectic month.

December Diane replaced her PC Jr. with IBM's new portable personal computer. She said it was heavy, suitcase-size and would fit in her car with her luggage, so planned to bring it when she came to Michigan for Christmas.

We got the children's Christmas toys finished and had made between five hundred and a thousand of each toy.

We had a nice Christmas dinner: thick slice of ham, sweet potatoes, cranberry sauce, salad, pumpkin pie with ice cream and an orange and apple to take back to our cells. Christmas meant so much to me now, not because of a good meal but because I finally had a fine family. God was good!

1986

January We heard that all across the country inmates were taking hostages. Things were edgy in Northside too. Three hostages were taken at Huron Valley prison and there was another stabbing in Central. We heard that men were hoarding food in case a riot broke out.

One evening, I was the only one at our group counseling session so was able to talk one-on-one with Dr. Klass. We talked about my past and where I was heading. I didn't tell him about the physical and sexual abuse from my stepfathers, however. *They called me bad as an excuse to justify my punishments. To them, I was just excess baggage.*

He suggested that friends and family write to the board on my behalf, and to let Senator Vaughn know what was happening. He also suggested that Pastor Settle tell the prosecutor that I held no ill feelings toward him.

Sharon, Chuck and Eric came to visit me. My little wiggly buddy Eric had gotten so tall!

February I got a copy of *Dog Fancy*, and saw my ad. It looked good, and I hoped for a lot of orders. Diane got the first order and we were on our way!

More shakedowns, so I began to clear my cell of my too-many projects. A guard stepped into my cell, looked at my woodworking, grinned, said "Come on, Otto, we're looking for all your weapons." Then he sat down and told me about his wife's craft work.

March Our Wood 'n Things orders were only dribbling in, and Diane and I were discouraged. She didn't like handling orders, so we decided it wasn't worth all the effort.

April I needed to make a major decision because Northside had gun towers and current state laws said it must become a maximum security facility. I did not want to be shipped out just anywhere and let the DOC decide for me. Barb came to see me and told me that Bruce (now her husband) loved it at Kinross. I talked with our block counselor about other prisons and he urged me to request a transfer soon. I called Diane and she agreed Kinross sounded like my best option, even though it was much further away. I put my name on the transfer list.

Things happened fast. I got the call: "Be ready to go in the morning." I got packed and disposed of my hobbycraft stuff (woodworking wasn't allowed at Kinross). Early the next day, I carried my belongings to the Control Center and had a quick breakfast before we boarded the bus. With stops along the way to let men off or on, we arrived in Kinross late at night, three hundred miles north of Jackson.

Before I left, Dr. Klass wrote his report for my file:

THERAPY TERMINATION REPORT

Mr. Bryan entered group psychotherapy for impulse control with me on 3/26/84 and continued until he was transferred on 4/18/86. This group met for ninety minute periods on a weekly-basis, and Mr. Bryan's attendance was regular and punctual.

One of the most active members of the group, Mr. Bryan was also one of the most questioning and direct. This directness was applied to his own dynamics and revealed surprising insight into his history of maladaptive behavior. An excellent historian, he gave a cogent account of early developmental events which led to, at times, a futile search for acceptance and identity. These events primarily involved a passive and seemingly rejecting mother figure and a succession of indifferent father figures. As a consequence, he has been on his own resources from an early age.

These resources, as measured by his accomplishments while incarcerated are substantial in regard to his intelligence, motivation, and goal direction. When he came to SPSM fourteen years ago, he was in a psychotic like state that required medication, and through the years, he has proven to be a disciplined, dependable individual capable of responsibility. The offense that sent him here was committed in a state of agitated depression and has been the subject of great remorse.

My contact with Mr. Bryan indicates that he is aware of the genesis of his combined feelings of rejection, guilt, and insecurity. Furthermore, I feel that he will be able to apply this insight into losses and rejections that he may yet suffer in his life.

Summarily, I feel that punishment has served its purpose. Incarceration, to any substantially greater length of time, may only serve to embitter or, in other ways, obliterate the progress he has made. He appears to have a caring wife and has considerable talent and positive future

plans. Some thought and planning for his
return to society may be appropriate.

Joseph Klass

Joseph Klass
Clinical Psychologist

Kincheloe (Kinross)

April 1986

I arrived at the "Kinross R&R Resort" and what a difference from the Jackson prisons. I ran around all day and was way behind on sleep. I saw a *real* doctor, not just a nurse. He ordered a bed board for me, renewed my Motrin®, said to see him if I had worse back pain and I'd get a full exam within a month.

The small town of Kinchloe was a former air force base in Michigan's Upper Peninsula and the prison buildings originally housed U.S. servicemen. The air field was now a small airport on the edge of town. Some of the prison employees lived in homes where Air Force families once lived.

I was housed in the gym and even there, the guards did their best to stay out of sight. I'd hear them laughing and joking with each other and watching us without interfering unless absolutely necessary. We had so much freedom. I saw guys I'd known over the years; it was almost a reunion of old friends. We could go outdoors most any time. Bruce walked me to death, until my legs screamed in protest. I wasn't used to all the space and loved it. Everyone moved in slow gear and it took me time to adjust.

The food was great and plentiful; I couldn't eat all mine. We'd have a meal, plus a loaded salad bar, as much as we wanted, plus milk *and* juice. It was not a "mess hall" but a "dining hall." There was no pushing or rushing and we had a choice of two dining halls.

The only hobbycraft done at Kinross was ceramics, with

a long waiting list. There were few jobs. I relaxed, didn't have to always watch over my shoulder and it felt like heaven after Jackson. I slept better too. All the fresh air, sunshine and quiet were wonderful.

Going North!   Going South!

There was always a wind so I came in looking like a bushman but felt close to God in this open place. One night I had to baby-sit my bunkmate because he got hold of some home-brew and was carried in by guards. The officer said if I could keep him quiet until he sobered up, he wouldn't get a ticket and go to the hole. He stayed quiet and was a decent man.

May I moved to the former bowling alley where about eighty men double-bunked. It was quieter and clean and I was near the showers. Here, each shower had a privacy door, which Jackson didn't. I hoped to eventually move into a three-man room where Bruce was. We were housed in separate buildings, rather than stacked together in one huge complex. The weather was good for Diane's first trip up here and after she left, I stretched out in the sun to watch a softball game with hot buttered popcorn. I felt like a human again!

June After the novelty of being in Kinross wore off, I was bored. I had nothing to do, and I wasn't the kind of man who wants to do nothing.

The overcrowded prisons in southern Michigan sent more men up here, and our big, once-quiet gym was noisy. Our bowling alley was filled up with bunk beds, plus more men in the warehouse. Mom and Dad came to see me on their way back from the west coast where they had taken a cruise to Alaska.

Diane was looking for rural wooded property near the Catskill Mountains in New York to build us a new home. I felt helpless, longing to be there and doing it with her. I needed to do something productive here. I couldn't do any artwork on my top bunk in the crowded bowling alley.

Chandra was working, taking college computer classes toward a degree and dating a young man, Rich. I hoped he liked camping. Kris had finished two years of college and moved into Diane's New York house too.

I moved into a three-man room with Bruce and Doug, and got a closet and desk with some working space. I slept like a baby the first night. It was quiet and dark and we had windows we could open or close and even watch the sun set. It had been years since I slept in a totally dark room. Yes sir, I was glad to be in Kinross.

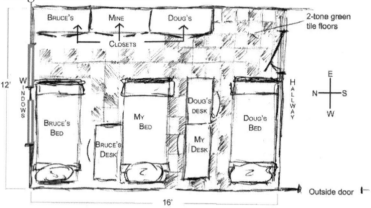

July Diane was here again. She'd found a small rustic rental cottage on the edge of town to stay in. I missed her as soon as she left. Our Fourth of July holiday picnic helped, however–I was stuffed!

Tempers got hot here too in our Paradise. Our quiet Kinross was becoming more like Northside... new young hot-heads arriving, and with them, fights. One man was cracked in the head with a padlock in a sock, another stabbed, then beaten with a board. Still, compared to Jackson, there was less tension and guards stayed in the background. I could walk outside and be alone if I wished.

Sharon and Chuck came to visit and I always enjoyed seeing them.

August Got some news about a possible resentencing for

lifers. Bruce's attorney told him it's great (for him, because he had no past record) but not for me (because of my past and serious crime). His attorney also said court judges were ignoring the ruling, rather than honoring it. I wished that positive things an inmate did while in prison would count more.

I thought about my arrest. After being picked up in Florida, riding two long days by car back to Michigan, I arrived at the county jail after midnight and was placed in an isolation cell. Early the next morning, the sheriff and undersheriff, an officer and the prosecutor grilled me to get their confession. I had no attorney (even though I'd asked for one), and didn't have one for quite a while after that. The paralegals here told me that the Michigan Supreme Court dismissed charges on at least thirteen people for this reason alone. I wished I had my court papers so I could look into it. Why hadn't Carter used that issue?

A large gander landed in our back field and explored the area for a couple of hours while we watched. We also had some resident groundhogs. It had been years since I've seen much wildlife (except for our Jackson riots where the only wildlife was men).

September I loved the openness here, especially the northern sky. I was out in the center of our field watching massive dark, ominous, rolling clouds coming in. In places, the bright sunlit sky shown. I knew a wall of hard rain would soon follow, but I couldn't make myself move. Half the sky was dark, the other had billowy clouds bathed in sunshine. I thought of the book of John where Jesus talked about coming out of the darkness and into the light. How could anyone see a sky like this and not know there was a God up there? Of course, by the time I got back to my unit, I was drenched. The guys teased me, but I didn't care; it was such an awe-filled sight.

October I decided to start researching in our law library; I didn't have much else to do and might learn something. I had

129

copies of some of my court papers, but none of the records kept by the judge and psych doctors that I wanted. I needed a typewriter to get into my case seriously.

Diane came and stayed in a cabin again, with her dog and portable computer. Work had started on her new house; the bulldozer had leveled the area for the foundation, and the footings were dug. I hated to see her leave again; our time together went by too fast.

I was going to the law library regularly, reading and searching through the manuals. The inmate paralegals told me I had some good issues to research. I wanted to find the current addresses of the psychiatrists I saw while in the forensic center so I could get their records. My legal issue checklist read like this:

✓ *Being held in solitary confinement in the county jail for 15 months.*

✓ *My audiotaped confession was not admissible because I didn't have an attorney present. There were no witnesses to my crime or of even being in the area, so my confession was the only evidence against me.*

✓ *My first attorney, O'Conner, was ineffective (didn't carry through); also I wasn't told I could plead not guilty by reason of insanity.*

✓ *I waived a jury trial before my competency was ruled on: I was found incompetent, was at the forensic center for over a year, and then was found competent. The sequence was askew.*

✓ *Medication alone could be reason to set aside my guilty plea and give me a new trial. I was on extremely high, probably experimental, doses of medications when I pled guilty:*
  • 5mg Artane 3x/day (for psychotic depression and tremors), the maximum dose.
  • 1000 mg chlorpromazine 1x/day (an anti-psychotic)
  • 100 mg amitriptyline or more 3x/day (an antidepressant). A total of 75 mg a day in divided doses is usually satisfactory but I had more, sometimes up to 300mg a day)

130

- ✓ *Due process and right to speedy trial (180 days) unless there was a good reason; did being in the forensic center count? I wasn't competent? I was mentally ill?.*
- ✓ *Using my past convictions to determine my sentence when I wasn't represented by an attorney.*
- ✓ *No copy of my Michigan arrest warrant among my legal papers*
- ✓ *The conditions of my arrest and county jail experiences were excessive.*

Diane wrote that she'd send me an early Christmas gift: money for a typewriter.

November Winter hit us. We had blowing snow, making it hard to stand upright or walk. During the evening, we turned off our lights so we could watch the storm out the window. I didn't go outside much, instead stayed in to read and work on my legal issues.

Diane took on the job as general contractor building our house and she often asked my advice. We shared all our ideas and my suggestions were important to her. She was the best friend I'd ever had. I admired her as well as loved her, was closer to her than I'd ever been to anyone.

I had a bad winter cold but once I felt better, I went back to work on my legal research. I didn't do badly for a novice. I learned that my taped confession wasn't admissible because the police took it after I requested an attorney (and one was not there) so was worthless because no one read it back to me, and I didn't sign or receive a copy of it. Was my guilty plea coerced by the fifteen months in isolation and my strong medications?

December My roommates Bruce, Doug and I were assigned jobs working in the kitchen for the month. Kinross lost quite a few kitchen workers because of transfers and holiday meals were coming up, which required extra help. We scraped and stacked dirty dishes for the dishwasher and worked fast to keep up with the busboys. I challenged myself to go even faster. My back muscles were sore, but it felt good to work again and be physically active. We earned a whole 10¢ an hour, 13¢ if we signed up for at least ninety days, which the three of us did.

I got my new electric typewriter, Diane's early gift, and Bruce and I enjoyed learning to use it.

The DOC was transferring men around, and I heard they wanted to put some of us lifers into Level 1 camps because we were the prison stabilizers who helped keep order.

Diane couldn't come for Christmas, so I was grateful that my job kept me from feeling sorry for myself. Besides the inmate kitchen, I volunteered to work on a banquet for the children in town. I enjoyed watching them have a good time in our dining hall. We had tinsel and bells decorating the hall and a big tree, but the children were the most excited about the pile of gifts under the tree. We wore clean white overalls with black ties. I really enjoyed being around the kids, but was exhausted afterward.

I got quite a few Christmas cards, seven in one evening. I felt blessed; and this year was too busy to have my usual holiday depression. On Christmas Day we had a terrific dinner—steak with mushrooms, baked potato with butter and sour cream, shrimp, cauliflower, hot rolls and pie with ice cream. We also got a lunch box of Christmas goodies for supper. Our kitchen crew also got a bag full of nuts and candy, oranges and bananas. Barb came to visit Bruce and after their visit, she stayed to visit me too.

1987

January I checked out some library books about landscaping and stonework and dreamed about fixing up the yard of our log house.

Doug and I had fun one day in our dining hall job. We shaped cake to look like a cooked rat and laid it on a plate in the serving line. It looked so real, it caused a big stir and the kitchen steward was all upset. No one caught us.

I went to the hospital in Sault Sainte Marie for an EKG;

my heart was healthy. Before I could get a new dental plate to replace my old one, I'd need mouth surgery in Jackson to rebuild my gum. I wasn't sure I wanted to go back there enough to get new dentures.

February An inmate was stabbed here nine times before he died. Kinross was not a quiet paradise anymore.

March Bruce's court hearing date was coming up soon so he left to go to the county jail in Detroit. I was hopeful for Bruce, that he'd get a break. A paralegal friend, Accord, moved into our room.

A female guard in Jackson was raped and strangled to death. A while ago, two female teachers were beaten and raped there. I worried about this sort of thing happening when women began working inside the all-male prisons. Even in Kinross, prison was a very stressful place to live and work. A thirty-seven year old at Kinross just died of a heart attack.

April Diane came to visit and brought photos of the half-built log house for me; my bulletin board was soon full. Our unit guard stopped in and looked at the photos and told me he'd like to build in a wooded setting like that.

Accord and I worked on my case together; he was a good roommate to have. He drafted some paperwork about my pleading guilty while on medication, and I mailed it to the local court. Cases moved faster through the northern courts than the southern. We passed step two (the magistrate). By the end of the month, I'd passed the third step. The magistrate wrote that I had some good constitutional issues, and he was waiting for the Attorney General's response. I prayed!

May Kinross added three hundred forty men here in one week, jamming in more partitions (called bulkheads) and more bunkbeds in all open areas like the gyms, shops and auditoriums. I envisioned trouble coming, as crowded as we already were. Last year we had room to roam around; no longer. It was still better than Jackson.

I called Mom and she told me Dad was doing better.

They decided to sell their big trailer and stop traveling with it.

Rumblings started; a federal judge told our governor not to build any new state prisons, instead to house inmates in county jails because Michigan prisons were overfilled. I wondered if we'd have rioting here. We were remote, so any state police or national guards had to be flown in to help. I hoped any riots here were only rumors.

June Bruce's judge postponed his decision again, and Barb was worn out from working in northern Michigan and traveling back and forth to court in Detroit. Diane was trying to get our log house finished so couldn't visit me that summer. Those two women drove a lot of miles for us men.

July Good news for Bruce! The judge reversed his conviction and Bruce was going home with Barbara. Meanwhile, I had to wait—the district court wanted an extension of time for my case.

August My friend Jesse got his reversal in court and was also going home. I was glad for him, but I still waited. *Lord, when will my time come?*

Chuck and Eric (then a teenager) went to New York to help Diane on the new house. Kris offered to handle the sale of the Poughkeepsie house, the new log house framework was up, and the plumbing and the electrical system going in. The back of the house faced south and was designed to be passive solar heated with large windows overlooking woods.

September Bruce was home, free, and came to see me on a visit. He looked great and said he and Barb were really happy.

October Diane and Kris moved into the new house just before a heavy snowfall, which left them with no electricity, heat or water for several days. That was one of the pitfalls of living in the country. Diane planned to get a wood stove and perhaps a generator too. *Lord, why am I still here and not home to help them?*

November Dad had another cancer surgery. I missed seeing the family and felt life was passing me by.

December Diane wasn't coming to Michigan for Christmas but spent it with the kids in the new house instead.

Doug had a trial date and the Circuit Court agreed to take Accord's case. My roommates were happy, but I still hadn't heard anything from the court. I was fifty; would I ever get home? If I got a reversal or dismissal of my conviction, I wondered if I'd have a cardiac arrest from the shock.

Our gym with bunks　　*Diane's Poughkeepsie home*　　*Back of our log home*
(watercolor paintings by Diane)

1988

January I mailed the last of my paperwork to the court and waited. The district judge had to either dismiss my suit or set a trial date and appoint me an attorney. No one was in a hurry to let me loose (except my family). I was frustrated that court rulings over the years stretched out sentences and added more restrictions. Waiting seemed endless; I had nothing else to challenge or help me feel productive.

I heard another guard was killed at Jackson. I hoped the DOC would crack down on the rules but not turn prisons into military-type settings that made them into "gladiator schools" that taught men to fight as Woodburn Reformatory did for us kids.

February I still waited for the court but, except for being separated from my family, I was content. Diane got another promotion and enjoyed our dream home; the kids were grown and successful on their own.

Our inmate population increased again at Kinross and so did trouble. A female guard scarcely escaped an attack, a male guard was beat up badly. There was a scuffle in the dining

135

hall, chairs knocked over, and food all over the floor. I was glad I no longer worked in the kitchen.

March I joked with my roommates and told them women couldn't resist my Irish charm. They teased me, said I was mentally ill and needed help. So I told them "I have court documents that claim I am legally sane. Do you?"

We had a thief on our floor. Someone got into our room by using his ID card to pop the door lock. Our radios, tokens, and a watch disappeared. Our rookie guards weren't watching.

April Spring-like weather, the seagulls and groundhogs were back and it was finally warm enough for Diane to travel here. I didn't know if I missed her more when I hadn't seen her for a long time or just after she left.

My young friend Larry whom I knew from SPSM wrote and sent me his phone number, so I called him. He was doing well, living in the Midwest, was married and happy.

My thumb was in a cast; it was broken when it got accidentally jammed in a door frame.

I finally got my ruling from the court. The magistrate said I didn't exhaust my state remedies first. I only had ten days to prepare and file an objection to the ruling. Most of my life I simply took the blame, fighting only when I absolutely had to. Now, getting home to my family was too important for me to drop my case. Bruce and Barb came to see me, and Barb encouraged me to keep up my efforts.

June The sixth circuit court of appeals accepted my case, so I could appeal to a higher court after my last dismissal. A friend suggested an attorney, James Lawrence, who he highly recommended. Diane said she'd sell some of her IBM stock to pay Lawrence's fee.

Mom wrote and invited me to stay with them if I got out on bond and had to stay in Michigan for a while. Chuck was pleased about Lawrence as my attorney and said he'd call him for me.

The cast came off my hand, then the doctor discovered I

also had a torn ligament. He stitched it up and put me back in another cast.

July Lawrence and I talked on the phone; he sounded sharp and sincere, and after researching my issues a little more, said he might take my case. He told me re-sentencing was a possibility and my good institutional record was a big plus, so I could be sentenced to "time served." That's what Bruce got. Lawrence said he knew both Judge Campbell and my former attorney, Carter. He asked me to send him the transcripts and reports I'd already gathered. He charged a thousand dollars to read, research and test the waters for a re-sentencing and said then we'd talk about his fee for taking my case further.

The second cast came off my hand and I exercised it until it got back to normal.

Accord was going to his court hearing and my transcripts were packed up, ready to mail to Lawrence.

One of the guards here who is very strict and always shaking men down took an interest in my roommates and me and made some nice remarks about me, the kind I used to hear in Central and Northside. When I dropped off my legal papers to mail to Lawrence, I saw him looking through them.

Later, while I was alone in our room, the guard came in, closed the door and sat down to talk. We discussed living in prison without family ties and how prison affected young men. He asked me about my feelings, my crime and hopes for the future. I showed him the few photos of my artwork that I had and he was impressed. Diane had put together a packet

for my court and parole efforts which, added to my list of accomplishments, was also pretty impressive.

I loaned the packet to him to read. When he brought it back, he said it sounded good, then asked about my crime and charges.

He said he didn't know how I was convicted with the

medicated condition of my mind and thought I should be released. After reading about me, he also said I should write a book. He was serious about it and told me that when I got home, to keep in touch with him.

With Accord gone and my case papers with Lawrence, I realized how much I needed to rest for a while. My new roommate, Brad, said he'd like to learn to draw, so I got creative again and said I'd teach him as long as he applied himself. My thumb was still wrapped, so I couldn't do much drawing myself.

August Upjohn announced its new "miracle hair growing" medicine, Rogaine® that I helped test three years ago. I still had scars on my arm to prove I was involved. Upjohn's stock doubled in value after their announcement.

Chuck and the boys were here to visit. Accord came back from court and asked me to research and type some legal materials for him. While he was in the Bay City jail, deputies beat him while he was handcuffed.

September It got cooler so I enjoyed being outdoors and seeing some color change in the trees. We heard that the DOC was going to put up Quonset huts on the grounds behind our gym and house two hundred more men here by the end of October.

Accord had a parole hearing this summer and was flopped, but promised another hearing next July if he attended therapy sessions. He refused to do it because he thought he'd have to admit his guilt and claimed he was not guilty. He was his own worst enemy. It had been four years since the parole board saw me, and if I were offered a chance like this, I'd jump at it. I talked to our counselor who told me that the board told counselors not to prepare any Parole Eligibility Reports (PERs) for lifers. He suggested I write a short and polite letter to them, bring it to him, he'd add some information to it and send it on to the board.

Chaplain Paulson, who used to visit me at SPSM, came to see me. He told me that at Jackson nearly all the prison programs were gone and no outside groups could come in with programs. They had a lot of 24-hour lockups too, which only bred trouble and hatred. No more common sense?

October Mom and Dad made a trip to New York; and I called to talk with them while they were at Diane's.

Accord and I are working on Doug's case now. I hoped Diane would bring a warm coat next time she came. We'd had a little snow already and the trees were almost bare.

November The weather stayed decent for Diane, then got really cold and windy after she was safely back home.

I was waiting to hear from Lawrence to see if he'd talked to Judge Campbell. I'd heard my judge had retired and was traveling. I was impressed with Lawrence even though we hadn't met in person. A fellow here (who didn't know that Lawrence was looking at my case) told us that Lawrence got a guy a substantial reduction in his time and also gave him half his money back because the case took less time than he'd expected.

I talked to Lawrence by phone and we had a long and interesting conversation. He was waiting for a response from Judge Campbell to the letter he'd written to him. He hoped Campbell would substantiate the conversation we'd had about sentencing me to life or a number of years. Campbell never denied the issue, so I was hopeful. Lawrence said even if Carter attested to the conversation, he wasn't actually there so the court would consider it hearsay.

I also asked Lawrence if he was able to look past the man I was seventeen years ago, and he assured me he could. He said he'd worked on worse crimes and records than mine. I was satisfied with that.

December While I waited for word from Lawrence, I still researched and read other cases. The more I read, the better I felt about my case. If I got a re-sentencing, a new judge must consider not only my past, but also the years that I'd been in prison. For me, that was good.

We got more than a foot of snow and extreme cold—it

felt like the arctic here even though we were thirteen hundred miles south of it. I really missed Diane and the family as Christmas approached.

Diane, Mom and Dad met with Judge Campbell at the Detroit airport where the judge and his wife were waiting for their flight to Florida. He agreed to write a letter to the board stating he had no objection to my parole. Even though he was retired, that was good! The year would end well with Lawrence on my case. Dad was doing well but getting forgetful.

A couple of new prison facilities just opened so men were being shipped out of Kinross and I was glad. Bruce came to visit me, said he and Barb were doing well.

As the year ended, we had about twenty inches of snow on the ground and more was predicted.

1989

January I was tired of moping around, feeling sorry for myself one minute–then angry the next. Lawrence had all my legal papers and I'd heard nothing. Did he consider my issues irrelevant? He did write me, but I didn't get his letter (although Diane got a copy). When she told me about it on the phone, I tracked it down in the mail room, and found out his letter had been returned to him, stamped with "Return to sender: Paroled." I told the mailroom I'd keep the envelope as proof I should be home.

When I finally got Lawrence's letter, I felt better. He had talked with Carter about his affidavit to re-sentence me. It was not great news but he was not giving up. Finally, someone was trying to get me home now that I was old enough to join AARP.

February Dad had a lot of pain and little energy again so might need more chemo.

March I had a bad week and lots of back pain again. I went to the Sault Sainte Marie for x-rays, but they found nothing serious. All I could do was take pain medication and stay in bed. Doug helped a lot to get me things I needed.

I prayed that Carter would come through when Lawrence saw him face-to-face. If a re-sentencing didn't happen, I might ask for a transfer to Coldwater to be nearer the folks. Dad's cancer had returned and he needed more treatment. Mom had high cholesterol and was on a trial medicine for that.

I talked to Lawrence on the phone. He cancelled his meeting with Carter because he had the flu and instead, had mailed Carter the affidavit to sign. Lawrence hadn't asked us yet for any payment for what he'd already done.

I got a dismissal on my "habe" in the federal court because I didn't appeal to the Michigan court of appeals first. A habe would allow me to bring my case from the state court into federal court, where I might have a better chance for release.

April Still no word; how long does it take Carter to sign his name to the affidavit? What was going on?

We had a stabbing in our unit, a guy's head was split open with a lock-in-a-sock, so guards went through our belongings looking for things that might be used as weapons. I was glad the weather was nice so I could get outside, to get away for a while.

Chandra had a new job, doing computer work for a law firm in Albany. She had grown up without me there.

Lawrence finally got the affidavit and met with Judge Michael Dodge (the former prosecutor for my case who was now the Cass County judge). Lawrence wanted to learn why I was charged with second degree and not first. Dodge said he didn't remember, but that I'd committed a horrible crime (which I didn't deny). They'd also suppressed my forensic reports that proved my mental state at the time of my crime, and O'Connor hadn't argued about that. I didn't ask the court to wipe out my conviction; I only wanted a new sentence to something less than "life."

May A vicious fight broke out in the dining hall; it was spaghetti night and what a mess!

I told Lawrence we should get the Florida arrest off my record. I'd pled guilty to that, so my life sentence was partially based on my being a fugitive, but I was technically a convicted felon instead. I also asked Lawrence if he should bring up the issue of my mental health at the time and the heavy medication I was on because those weren't considered at my sentencing. If I lost my fight again, I was afraid I'd lose Diane. Would she stick with me?

I talked to our counselor about transferring to Lakeland in Coldwater. It would be closer to the folks, and Dad's condition was getting worse, so I could request a family hardship transfer. It was also the closest state prison to Cassopolis if I needed to go back to court.

Accord and I worked hard to gather case laws that might help Lawrence. I wanted to go ahead; his $4,000 fee was reasonable. He didn't want to attack my guilty plea—I *was* guilty, I didn't deny that. I wanted to fight about the incompetence of my trial attorney, O'Connor, and the judge, in sentencing me to life for a second-degree charge. 'Life' was reserved for first-degree, premeditated murder and mine was not premeditated.

The folks went to New York to visit Diane and the kids; I wished I were there too. Family meant everything to me, and if I lost them, I'd be back where I was most of my life— alone and bitter. I never wanted to go back to that again! I remembered my loneliness, the hurt inside that distorted my outlook so that I put on a false front. I guess some people grow up alone and end up just fine. I didn't know how to do that; I needed a family to make my life meaningful.

June Dad's doctor wrote a hardship letter to the DOC and Mom sent me a copy. His illness could put me on the transfer list. Once I was at Coldwater, I'd have to start all over, living first in a gym then eventually get into a room. It was time for me to go back south.

July Diane came to visit, and it helped my time waiting

142

for a transfer to go by faster. Dad was feeling better, which was good news.

Diane had sent me a lot of new photos of the house, and I dreamed of being there. I sat outside under a tree and talked with friends about what I might want to do with our yard. Diane wrote that Kris was working fulltime for Texaco and going back to college to finish his business degree; I was glad about that.

Before the end of the month, I packed up for Coldwater and sent Diane a quick note that I was leaving Kinross.

Coldwater (Lakeland)

July 1989

Lakeland, my new home in Coldwater, had been a state home for the disabled. Lakeland was smaller than Kinross, with only six hundred fifty men, plus two small geriatric units. There was a large yard with a few trees, and I could see the woods beyond our fence. Other than walking in the yard, I didn't have much to do, except write long letters to Diane. We both did that anyway, and had since we first met.

I bunked in the dayroom and it was hot and uncomfortable. I had to throw away some things, as we were only allowed what fit in our footlocker and a narrow locker. An officer said if I kept everything inside my lockers and stayed ticket-free, I could probably move to the cube area in a few weeks.

I escaped the noise by walking outdoors as much as I could. I met an old man there who had been in prison since 1940; he was the last surviving member of the infamous Purple Gang that terrorized Detroit during the '30s.

August I wrote to Chuck and Mom and asked them not to visit me here until the end of the month because I had to guard my property and keep it locked up. A new friend, Greg, and I watched out for each other, but someone still managed to steal $5 from him.

I wanted to walk out of here a free man; I was waiting for news from my attorney, Lawrence.

Walking laps was a good time for me to talk to the Lord,

144

thanking him for my family and taking care of me through some dangerous situations in prison. I also prayed He'd let me go home. I was feeling good inside, planning for the future. Such a change from my early life, when I just wandered aimlessly around.

I talked to Mom on the phone and told her how much I appreciated Diane for waiting so long and that it meant a great deal that the family accepted me. Mom said, "That isn't hard to do–you're a very likable man."

September I called Lawrence; he was working on my brief and planned to set a hearing date with a judge. I hoped it would go quickly and as planned. My Kinross friend, Spalla, arrived here yesterday; he's the man who recommended Lawrence to me. Another friend, Skinner, asked me about Christianity and wanted to learn more. We had a good talk and later I saw him reading a bible.

Lawrence sent me a copy of my brief. Spalla read it and said "I tell you, Otto, you are going home! This is even better than I thought."

Diane finished adding a garage with a large studio over it to our house and sent me a copy of her watercolor of it.

October Diane came to visit and, as always, I hated to see her leave. God willing, it would be our last prison visit until I went home. It had been over sixteen months since I first contacted Lawrence, and I wished things moved faster.

I saw my friend Big Red one morning. He'd just come from Kinross. He was a big man–not fat, just big–and good to have as a friend. None of the guys would dare take him on.

One inmate here attacked a guy with a pool cue, destroyed his eye and split his head. I was just coming inside when the attacker was handcuffed and surrounded by a half dozen guards.

I was finally number one on the list for a cube and on moving day, all I had to carry was my clothes on hangers. Other guys swooped in to help carry everything else into the much quieter cube area.

Diane took a business trip to California and added some vacation days to visit her cousin there. She asked if I'd like her to search for some of my family while she was on the west coast. I said no, I'd like to know how my mom was doing, but my real family lived in New York and Michigan.

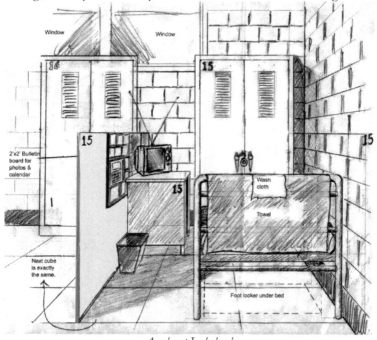

A cube at Lakeland

November I marked the days off on my calendar for my hearing date, December 18. If the judge ruled in my favor, I'd be resentenced and go right home. An officer asked if I wanted to work in the inmate store, but I didn't. In that job some workers often stole and everyone who worked there got blamed. I wanted my record to remain clear.

December I called and talked to Mom. Dad had been groggy and tired. His doctor gave him some pills so he could enjoy Christmas while Diane was there.

My hearing was postponed because the prosecutor wanted an extension. Spalla reminded me that if the prosecutor didn't answer my brief, he'd lose the right to argue against me and the court could rule in my favor.

1990

January New year, more changes. No longer could anyone send stamps to us; we had to buy them through the prison store. Money could come only from family members, so we worked it out. If I needed to repay someone here, Diane sent a money order to his family, who could then send it to him. It took longer, but worked.

Over the past few years, the MDOC cut one thing after another. No more college or vocational training, and personal clothes and items were limited. Most jobs and hobbycraft programs were gone, no hobbycraft store to sell our work like we'd had at SPSM. Even legal research was limited. My time dragged.

Diane ordered a self-study course on cassette tapes for me about real estate and buying income properties. Even if I never did it, just learning about the real estate business gave me a lift and kept my mind busy. Where would I be without Diane? She'd motivated me to get my life together. I called Lawrence, who hoped to convince the judge that I deserved a lesser sentence. He'd scheduled a telephone conference call.

February Mom and Dad came to see me after visiting Dad's sister and her husband who lived in Coldwater.

My hearing was held, my motion denied. My heart was so heavy, I could hardly think. Lawrence sent me this report:

Hearing held before Judge William C. Buhl; motion was orally denied. No evidentiary hearing held (as requested). Written order denying motion signed 2/20/1990.

Looking at this file, it appears to me that the appellate counsel fought tooth and

147

nail and certainly earned the court-
appointment counsel fee ten times over and
made a recommendation which, assuming it is
true and that he made it and it was relied
upon, cannot be said to be a critical
error, taking all things into
consideration.

My ineffective counsel charge was dismissed, but I knew Lawrence did his very best for me. He'd told me there were other issues that we could pursue. I stayed buried in my real estate course and felt more hurt than angry about the judge's ruling. Sharon and Chuck came to see me and that helped my mood. I told them "I really love this family." Sharon reached over, squeezed my hand and said "We all love you, too, Otto." How did I deserve them?

March I almost got a ticket. A guard came in for a shakedown and found the used tape player I had bought in Kinross from a guy who was leaving. I'd scraped off his number and etched in mine. The guard asked if I had the paperwork on it (and I didn't). He said because I'd never been a problem, he'd overlook this. I knew I'd better get rid of the player, in case someone else did my next shakedown. I listened to the radio and tapes all the time, so ordered a new tape player. I hated to ask Diane to pay for it, but had no way to earn money here.

April Our counselor put in a good word for me to the Quartermaster for a job—told them I was no trouble, respectful, and always tried to do something productive with my time. The Quartermaster's office handled inmates' prison clothing, bedding and other prison supplies. Each time we were transferred to another prison, we turned in our prison uniforms and bedding and got replacements when we arrived at the next one.

I thought about starting a small mail order business selling informational booklets about how to make toys like I made at Jackson. I could write directions and draw the pictures. The only problems were that I could no longer

148

order the felt-tip drawing pens and I'd need someone outside the prison to handle orders.

June I had a visit with Mom and Diane's cousin, Pat. Pat asked to hear how I'd found the Lord. I smiled, said "I didn't find Him, He found me" and told her about the Bible in the county jail cell. We prayed together before they left and afterwards, I cried, thankful for the visit that reminded me of God's great love for me.

I saw our unit counselor who told me that lifers were not being paroled but there was some hope coming. The MDOC was under pressure to cut costs and releasing men like me was one way to do that. He pointed out that I'd met all the requirements of therapy, finished my GED, took some college classes and had good unit and work reports.

July Sharon, Chuck and the boys came to visit me on the Fourth. That night we watched fireworks in town through the prison fence.

All my life, I never had enough money for what I had to buy, little things like soap or underwear. In prison, I needed art materials too. I thought a multi-level (pyramid) sales idea might earn me some easy money. I got busy working on a "business opportunity program" based on re-distributing mailing lists. I'd need someone outside (maybe Diane) to help with things I couldn't do from prison, like mailing information and receiving payments. I wrote her about my idea.

August Diane wrote that she was not comfortable helping with my little "business opportunity" because she thought pyramid schemes were a bit dishonest. She was right, as always, but I was desperate to get something going and not be dependent on the family. It wasn't fair that they had to support me.

Years ago in prison, I was so stressed that I ground my teeth down and I was on the list for new dentures. I'd nearly broken my lower dental plate just before Mom and Dad came. I couldn't turn down a visit with them, in spite of it.

Dad was looking good and felt better.

November The district court dismissed my case about being kept in solitary at the jail. It didn't seem fair, but I was relieved that I'd tried and it was over.

Diane visited at Thanksgiving with Kris, Chandra and her fiancé, Rich. I missed them before they even left Michigan. I felt ashamed that my future son-in-law had to meet me in prison.

After they left, I was discouraged. Another holiday had gone by with me still in prison. I almost quit believing God would help me. There were no productive or creative things for me to do at Lakeland. I couldn't get a job, even with my work experiences. Just do my time, week by week, month by month, year by year and continue to waste time. Had God forgotten me?

December I called Diane and was pleased that she and the kids were coming to Michigan for Christmas. Christmas was always better when my family was near. After they left, no mail went in or out until January, so the last week of December dragged by until Mom and Dad came to visit on their way to see family in Coldwater.

1991

January We hoped changes would come with a new governor in office. He issued a stop order for building three new prisons and talked about closing three others. Some of us would have to be released.

We also heard rumors the governor might abolish the parole board and rule that we're eligible for release after serving one third of our sentence. That meant that I'd still have a chance for release. However, because my sentence was "life" the board couldn't divide "life" into thirds. I'd still need a change to a number of years.

We had more layoffs in the DOC; some counselors and administrators had to leave.

February A new approved typewriter list came out; I liked the $384 Canon electric one. Diane needed a new car, so I didn't want to ask her for money, but she sent it anyway. I ordered the typewriter. Maybe she was tired of reading my handwritten letters?

One of our guards came from the Cassopolis area, where my trial was held. He caught me up on the Cass County news. One judge was forced to retire, another disbarred. The assistant prosecutor was fired for bribing witnesses. The sheriff was busted for fraud, and the undersheriff killed himself. One of the guards who brought me back from Florida was fired, and my two jailers drank themselves to death. The only person still all right was Sergeant Parrish, who had given me the old Bible in jail.

We had a major shakedown when someone stole an inmate's work putty knife. The guard who checked my cube made only a pretense of it.

Word went around that the "goon squad" (the harshest guards) killed an inmate named Oso. Things were tense; guards barked orders, inmates ignored them and wore arm bands in protest. We heard that Oso had been handcuffed, carried face down then dragged in the snow and mud. Guards dropped him, and one knelt with his knee on Oso's throat. Oso wasn't moving, so another guard took his pulse and ran for a stretcher to take him to health services. They said that he'd had a heart attack. He was only twenty five and healthy as a horse.

Later, four of the guards were suspended with pay. Instead of a heart attack, they claimed Oso had a rubber glove filled with marijuana and attempted to swallow it, then choked to death. The state police talked to witnesses who said the guards rammed Oso's head into a sink and wall. Someone took photos and recorded the scene on a camcorder. Tensions remained high, and those of us wearing arm bands got thorough shakedowns. If a guard was killed, all the guards wore black arm bands. Why couldn't we show respect for a fellow inmate's death? I wore one, not only for

151

Oso, but also for a young guard who had recently died in an auto accident. Oso's family brought in a doctor and attorney to attend his autopsy. The coroner said his body was covered with bruises around his neck and ribs where he'd been repeatedly kicked. The family filed a suit against the guards and the DOC.

March An old friend from SMSP, Drobil, arrived here. He told me his wife was part of a nonprofit organization working on prison conditions called MI-CURE. Drobil suggested I send them one of the information packets that Diane and I had put together for the parole board. MI-CURE might help me get home.

Lawrence sent me the State Supreme Court ruling and, as expected, they also turned me down. He said I could go through the federal district court, and his fee for that was $3,000. I didn't want Diane to pay more, so had a good talk with the Lord and asked Him, "Should I give up on getting out and going home? Or, am I just tired of struggling?" He didn't answer. It was a lot of money, and Diane had Chandra and Rich's wedding coming up. However, she insisted Lawrence should go ahead and she would take money from her savings.

The governor did not do away with the parole board as we'd hoped; instead, he added three new members.

May I thought about printing and selling informational or how-to booklets. I'd have to do research from inside prison and get art materials in spite of the rules, just to prove I could. I had the new typewriter and could draw illustrations with a cheap ballpoint pen. I'd be happy to be doing something, if someone could handle mailing and collecting money for me. Again–Diane didn't want to handle sales. She worked long hours and explained to me that as a kid, she was shy and failed at selling personalized Christmas cards door-to-door and never wanted to do it again. She also said she wasn't good at keeping records or bookkeeping and was afraid she'd mess up things. I had to give up that idea.

June The new MDOC director and his staff came to look at Lakeland on a very hot day. We had to scrub, polish and buff everything. The only places they went, however, were the mess hall, health services and geriatric center–all air conditioned. The MDOC had to cut costs; closing prisons and laying off staff was one way. Instead, they just cut down our food rations and limited our toilet paper.

July I drew a picture for Diane of some of the river-worn stone heads I used to make. I wondered if stones would work for chess pieces, so did some sketches.

River Worn Stones   *Chess piece ideas*

I had a nice visit with my whole Michigan family–Mom, Dad, Chuck, Sharon and the kids, Kurt and Eric.

August I made a little money selling my handmade greeting cards for $1.50 each. I had a good fine-line drawing pen after an officer slipped me one.

Lawrence filed for a new trial with the federal court because O'Connor should have argued for a sentence of a number of years rather than life at my sentencing. It should go faster than it did in the state court, though Lawrence warned me it could take a year or two. I remember that Judge Campbell told me, "Otto, keep a clean record and you can be released after ten years." Unfortunately, that didn't appear in my court transcripts. Instead, my sentencing transcript said

153

that the prosecutor, Mr. Dodge, based on my past record, recommended that I be committed to prison for the rest of my natural life. I'd never seen my transcripts, so didn't know that the courts and parole board based their decisions on what the prosecutor wanted, not the judge.

Diane was busy with Chandra's wedding preparations and making dresses for Chandra and her two bridesmaids. They planned a garden wedding at Rich's folks' house.

September For Labor Day, we had the best meal I'd had since getting here: thick and tender steak, salad, peas, buns and banana pudding for dessert. On the way out we got two apples and an orange.

All the family went to New York for Chandra and Rich's wedding. I wished I was there too. Diane sent me some wedding pictures; it was a lovely setting.

November Diane got me a new warm coat and vest for winter.

A fellow in our unit died last evening; he was only forty-three years old. Lord, I'd hate to die while still in prison.

Got good news from Lawrence. My case would not be subject to a summary dismissal; the prosecution had to file an answer. I wrote to thank him.

What became dangerous contraband here? Pennies and 1¢ stamps.

December We went outside to romp in the six inches of snow we got. It was snowing hard, we couldn't see five feet ahead but had fun, then came in to sip some eggnog that the prison store had just added as Christmas goodies we could buy.

I was busy making Christmas cards and stationery. I collected $45 last draw day, with orders for more cards. I decided to start making Valentine cards after Christmas.

Diane was at the folks' for Christmas, so I called and talked to all the family and Chuck's mother, Esther, who had flown up from Florida.

My hobbycraft order arrived and included the set of drawing pens that I'd ordered but never expected to get. That was followed by a visit with Diane. Being with her was a perfect ending to my year.

1992

January Two state senators wanted Lakeland closed and our warden was hot about it, sick of the rumors. I'd heard that the average cost per inmate at Lakeland was $55 a day, $6 less than any of the other western Michigan prisons. The MDOC wanted at least one hundred fifty more men housed here. I'd gladly volunteer to go home to my family to give them one more bed space.

My new friend, Randy, ordered some card stock, felt tips and colored pencils, so I kidded him about setting up a card business to compete with me. He said he ordered art supplies because he hoped I'd teach him to draw, and I said I would. I got the rest of my order, scissors and card stock, all set for making more cards and glad I had good drawing pens.

February Randy and I pooled our money, fixed and shared a big batch of macaroni salad.

Something was going on here–we all got new photos and ID cards and got our health files brought up to date. Health services listed that I had chronic obstructive pulmonary disease (COPD), for some reason. My only complaint was my aching back.

Rumors were that Lakeland would become a women's prison, and we'd all be transferred somewhere else. I hoped my court issue was over before I had to transfer so I wouldn't have to begin the process in a new district. The Attorney General's time extension soon would run out, and I didn't have good news to tell Diane yet.

The MDOC planned to hold a public meeting about new prison rules to restrict our TVs and personal clothing. Inmates were not happy. Changes were being made to our housing, removing the plywood half-walls between our cubes and replacing them with concrete block walls. What was going on?

A guy here, Vargas, said he may be released after twenty years. He'd gotten a lot of tickets in prison, but told me he was re-sentenced because "no one was killed." He still had to face the parole board, so it wasn't positive he'd go home soon. I had a clean record and was still here. Why him and not me, Lord?

Randy fixed us some macaroni salad again; I joked that I'd gained weight from his cooking.

At the end of the month, Lawrence told me the Attorney General had filed for another extension, and he expected the judge to grant it. More waiting…

March The judge gave the prosecutor an extension to April, as we'd expected.

Three guys went to the hole last evening for planning an escape over the fence, and someone snitched on them. I heard that at the Adrian prison five young lifers tried to escape. They stole a truck and rammed it through the gate. One was shot at the gate, two were captured right outside, and the other two caught after running out of gas. Trying to escape was a dumb thing to do; it rarely worked, you were transferred to Level 5 and given more years to serve.

Space got tighter, and our health services were cut to a physician's assistant, traveling dentist, a few nurses and less equipment. I wondered if visits would be cut too. I'd put my name on a list to move into a room, to bunk with a new friend, Flores. Randy was leaving soon and I'd miss him.

Demolition Day arrived and all our furniture was shoved into the middle of the room. A crew tore out the plywood half-walls and marked the floor for cinder-block ones.

Only three days until the court looked at my sentencing issue again, and I was anxious about it.

April My copy of the attorney general's brief arrived and it wasn't good. I wrote to Lawrence that the attorney general should have admitted O'Connor made an error. I also pointed out that the attorney general said I missed filing an appeal within the sixty-day time limit. I was locked up in the SPSM psychiatric unit for several months after I started serving my sentence, so couldn't file from there.

When the guards changed shifts, an officer walked up to me and said loudly, "Otto, I'm sorry I ran off with your pen yesterday ... here it is." He handed me two new very good drawing pens so I could get back to serious artwork again. Some of the guards treated us as fellow humans, not just inmates, and I was grateful.

I began making Easter cards for spending money. I didn't sell many, but I inspired other guys interested in learning to draw. Maybe we'd get an art class here?

A guy hid his shank near my window and when I found it, he tried to become my friend. I told him he'd pulled a dirty trick on me that could have caused me a ticket, time in the hole and a black mark on my record. His eyes teared up, and he said he was really sorry. I forgave him and we both felt better, but I couldn't trust him as a friend.

I called and talked to Dad, who asked how my legal case

was going. For the first time, he said he'd be glad to see me go home. I loved him for saying that. If I'd had a dad like him who cared about what happened to me, I'd be different and not in prison. Knowing Dad, and the kind of father he was to Diane and her sisters, helped me understand a father's love and to trust God the father in a way I never could before.

A forty-four year old here died of a heart attack, which reminded me to get more exercise.

I wrote a long letter to Lois. The Dankers never gave up on me. For a long time, I didn't trust them; after all, no one had ever cared about me before them. Once I met Jesus and realized how much he loved me, I was able to trust the Dankers. At my very worst, somehow they saw something good in me. I'll always be grateful.

May I made Mother's Day cards–and even helped my competition. Guys came and asked how to draw something and I'd show them. Then they traced or copied my example onto a card that they would sell. I liked to help, so wasn't really angry with them.

Diane was here again for our anniversary. She still believed in me and stuck with me all these years. I'd never loved anyone the way I loved her. God knew I needed someone to soften my heart. Sharon and Chuck came to visit too.

I moved into a two-man room with my friend Flores at the end of a hall. The guard said he wanted guys there he could trust. We had two large windows we left open at night and grew plants on the sills and on top of our lockers. Because it was quiet, Flo could watch TV while I listened to the radio in the opposite corner. Our room was one of the few honor rooms at Lakeland. We had 24-hour power, so could keep lights and radios on all night. Flo was a good man to have on my side; he was trustworthy and could bench-press 445 lbs.

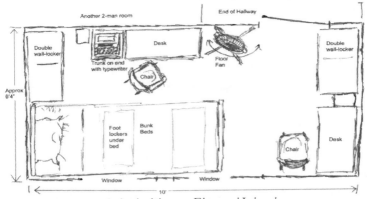

A sketch of the room Flores and I shared

A paralegal, Bill, asked to see my legal paperwork; he told me, "You're going home, Otto!" I felt great about Bill's comments, but still had no official word from the court.

A guard came by our room and said, "Want to see something funny?" An inmate was caught in the razor wire on the top of the fence with a crowd of guards standing around watching. It took an hour to cut him down. Turned out he was drunk on some homemade juice and decided to go home. Poor guy—five years tacked onto his sentence for an attempted escape, and he went back to a maximum security prison.

Newspapers reported that an inmate named Williams (whom I knew at Jackson) was released on parole, then abducted a woman and put her into his car trunk. Someone saw him and called the police. The woman was not hurt, but police learned Williams had done that before, taking women to a wooded area, killing and burying them there. Police found four bodies. There was a big uproar and officials blamed the parole board. I was so sick of being on the wrong side of the law.

The parole board wanted to see Flores again. He was a good man and I'd be glad for him if he were released.

June I had a bad allergy or cold that made my chest sore from coughing, fluid gurgling in my chest and my ribs ached. Health services just replied: "You'll be seen in one to two

159

weeks." I felt like I was dying.

I called Diane (who wasn't home), then Barb and soon an officer told me to get to health services right away. Seems that Barb had called health services to tell them I was very ill. Barb was very good at getting things done. The physician's assistant put me on the list to see the doctor, gave me antibiotics and told me to buy allergy medicine at our inmate store. I took all the medicines, yet still had sore ribs from coughing. The doctor finally prescribed a nasal spray and stronger antibiotics.

July We celebrated the Fourth with good food, an omelet-and-pancake brunch, with steak, potato salad and corn-on-the-cob for supper.

One night I helped Flores clean up the kitchen where he worked as a cook. When we were done, we chomped down on foot-long pieces of fried catfish he fixed for us and the kitchen supervisor. It was nice to have a cellmate who cooked.

Before Diane came for her next visit, I hoped to have a positive decision from the judge so we could celebrate.

August I was numb. Got the judge's decision–he turned down a re-sentencing, and blamed me for waiting nineteen years to appeal. I was concerned about how Diane would take it and guilty about putting her though all my disappointments again and again. I didn't deserve her love. Maybe she'd be better off if she divorced me?

I was angry at the judge, the rotten justice system, being blamed for the state's violation of my rights and mostly at myself. I felt guilty because I'd never complained that Carter did nothing. Then I remembered that I killed the Rodericks and felt the court was justified in locking me up forever.

I would not give up. Yes, the courts could stop me from going home and the MDOC could stop me from being productive but they could not stop me from using my mind. I couldn't make wooden products, but I could draw and sell plans for them. I sketched some wooden garden whirligig

160

ideas that I'd like to make to sell some day.

Diane reassured me she loved me and would stick by me, no matter what. She told me love didn't give up on people. I had faith that our Lord would bring our family together because I still had the possibility of parole.

One of the officers got me some big sheets of paper, so I began working on full scale woodworking plans, perhaps to sell to woodworking magazines. Two officers said they'd buy my plans if they were for sale.

September Flores' supervisor sent another guard to see my plans. He asked me, "You mean you do all that just in your head?"

I answered, "Yes, that is what I do, woodworking without any wood. I mentally build things, go through all the steps, illustrate them in my mind and then draw them on paper."

We had constant transfers in and out of Lakeland. There were only a few guys that I still knew. I did learn that MI-CURE didn't help to release men; instead, they worked to better prison conditions.

October Because the DOC needed to house more inmates, the governor told the parole board to hold at least five lifer hearings at every prison and to consider lifers who had served twenty-plus years with clean institutional records. I had nearly twenty in. One bad thing: lifers not selected must wait five years for their next reviews.

November Flores came back from his board hearing very angry. No updates were in his file and the parole member he saw had no record of his past reviews, work reports or therapy. The counselor talked to the board member, told Flo to submit the new information and wait to get his parole decision. We should get medals for waiting.

I got some good news from the court–I was in the running again. Lawrence had convinced the judge my issue was not frivolous. That was a great early Christmas present so I wrote to everyone.

Then, a week later, I was turned down again because of a procedural default in my case. I know Lawrence did his very best for me. Flores helped calm me down.

I didn't know how to tell Diane, so I poured out my feelings in a drawing for her that I called *Isaiah 53:1*.

But He was wounded for our transgressions, He was bruised for our iniquities. The chastisement for our peace was upon Him and by His stripes we are healed.
Isaiah 53:1

I was more concerned about how Diane felt than about myself. As a new Christian, I remembered praying for a loving heart and Jesus gave me that. Sometimes it hurt.

Flores helped me pull together, like I'd helped him. Talking with Diane helped too. She was still completely behind me. *This was so unfair to her. I'm not worthy of her or the family. I'm such a failure. I'm becoming bitter and I didn't want to be. God, why did you allow me to hope, but then say "wait?"*

It was hard, but I wrote to family and friends about the decision and thanked them for praying. Any time we had a setback like this, I was more concerned about how Diane felt than about myself; and at the same time, Diane was mostly concerned about how I felt. We had the kind of Biblical love for each other Paul wrote about in I Corinthians 13:7 "Bears all things, believes all things, hopes all things, endures all things."

December Encouraged to keep going, I ordered some good drawing supplies. Flo had ordered a bunch of Popsicle sticks, then didn't know what to do with them, so I designed him a cute Adirondack chair with a pin cushion in the seat.

162

He made them to sell to inmates to give as Christmas gifts.

All the family was in Michigan at Mom and Dad's on Christmas Day so I called. We had a nice brunch here, and for dinner, a whole rack of beef ribs, really good and more than most of us could eat. We got baked potatoes, chef salad, eggnog, banana cream pie and left with a bag full of holiday goodies.

A new year was coming, so I reflected on what to do next. In my early years at Jackson I concentrated on serious art. The Lord took care of me and led me to people who encouraged me. Best of all, He brought me Diane because of it. I decided to get back to doing serious artwork.

1993

January Flores saw the board again last week; we both hoped he'd leave before long. He'd served fourteen years, was getting anxious and his family was waiting. But he was turned down again. I tried to cheer him up by getting him to watch football while we rooted for different teams, rolled up tortillas and joked about it—but he still felt bad. I understood.

The DOC asked for volunteers to go to a new facility near Flint. It was closer for the folks, but if I had further legal action, I didn't want to transfer to another court.

February I was bored and still played around with whirlygig plans, but had started nothing serious. One of the guards who did woodworking said he'd like to take me home with him on weekends so I could work in his shop. I'd love that.

March We had snow piled high along our walkways, and I couldn't see ten feet ahead but went outside to walk around. It felt good to be alone with my thoughts of being home to help Diane dig out of the snow, then sitting by the woodstove having cocoa, with the dogs curled up nearby...

I enjoyed two visits this month. One was with Mom and Dad. Dad felt good and was fairly chipper. My other visit was with Chuck, Sharon and Kurt. Sharon reminded me so much

163

of Diane in her mannerisms and looked a lot like Mom.

April I got a letter from the Dankers; they were going to Europe in May. Fred had just finished writing a thousand-page Greek Lexicon of the New Testament. He was seventy-three, still writing and lecturing.

May Diane was in Michigan for our anniversary again. She's loved me, believed in me, and stuck with me for seventeen years. God knew I needed someone like her to soften and re-shape this old heart of mine.

June Heard that a friend just a year older than me died in prison of liver cancer.

July A young inmate, Kenny, became a friend. He was from England and had been arrested in Michigan on a visit. He tagged along and started making laps with me and then nearly every time I left my room, he was right there. He was a Christian and hoped to be deported back to England before long.

August Diane was here and gone. Our time together passed too quickly. She had really enjoyed the multimedia projects she did at work. I'd love to do that too. A few days after she left, I waited in the phone line, where guys teased me...

"Hey, Otto, who you calling?"

"I'm calling home, just so my wife won't forget who the boss is."

"Yeah, right! We know who the boss is..."

"Just wait and see..."

Then they kept cutting me off before I could dial. We had fun and they finally let me call Diane.

SPSM closed down because of some sort of fast-spreading virus. We heard two men had died, eight others were in the hospital with something serious. I remembered how bad the water smelled there, like sewage at times, and the plumbing was very old. The inmate plumbers didn't always know what they were doing.

September Latest news from SPSM: four dead, thirty-three others in serious condition. It was in the air-circulation system on the roof, not something in the water, and turned out to be Legionnaires disease. We heard that the virus had spread to Kinross and one of the guards died; the MDOC had kept transferring men around, germs and all.

October The month dragged on. Flores was waiting for his next parole hearing, and I hoped to have a parole hearing by the end of the year too.

November Flores came back from his parole board meeting very angry. The board member had no record of his past reviews, work reports or therapy. The counselor talked to the board member, then told Flo that with the new information, he should get his parole. More waiting.

Two fellows died here, one was forty-four, the other sixty-three and both had heart problems.

I had too much greeting card competition, so designed Christmas stationary sheets with matching envelopes instead for inmates who wanted to write special letters.

My young friend Kenny was slashed in the stomach by three guys. Kenny had refused to give them the credit card number he used to call his family in England. Kenny was going home soon and I hoped he'd be safe until then.

The board turned down Flores' parole again. His review was a big fiasco. The reason: "poor prognosis." How could he fix that? The board was not supposed to use catch-all phrases like that. The counselor and Deputy Warden were surprised, too. I wished I could help, so I suggested Flo put together a parole packet, similar to the one that Diane and I had done for me, pointing out what he's done during his prison time and then send it, with a request for a re-hearing, to the board.

I worked as a volunteer in the Quartermaster's for a couple days to move shelving around. I'd heard one of the paid workers might go home before long, so there could be an opening. The supervisor, Connie, seemed nice.

December Connie asked me to join the crew when the

165

prison newspaper photographer came to take a photo. My friend Wally, who had recommended me, said Connie liked me and thought I'd fit in well. Pay was $1.46 a day, one of Coldwater's highest wages, a lot of hard work, but it was something to feel good about. I'd have to account for everything going in or out of the prison, even discards, plus keep track of all the supplies for the laundry. I was good at organizing, and could learn to keep their records as well as I tracked my own money and supplies. Connie said I could set the storeroom up any way I wanted.

We had a bit of fun with one inmate, Taylor. Diane had sent me some brand new bright red undershorts as a joke, so I got some fabric paint, put a heart on the shorts with the words "LUV U." Then I  had friends' add their names around the heart. Connie helped to pack and label it as something she'd received at Quartermaster's, and put Taylor on call to pick it up. She told him she'd lost the mailing slip so didn't know who sent it.

Taylor came to each of us who had signed the shorts, but we all denied knowing anything. In the mess hall, one of the guys told the sergeant that it appeared as if Taylor was hiding something in his pocket. The sergeant pulled him over for a shakedown in front of everyone, held up the shorts and said "What's this?" while we all roared. Taylor was a good sport, but I hoped he didn't find out that I was the one behind our prank.

I didn't get called for a parole hearing, but Connie offered me the Quartermaster job. The job would pay for my art materials, and was a good way to end my year.

1994

January I got all of the new art supplies I'd ordered plus had collected old sponges, toothbrushes, shaving brushes and popsicle sticks to create textures. I drew rocks for fourteen hours over a weekend, rocks that I saw only in my mind. Time buzzed by as I felt that was what I was born to do. I also started some other drawings that I saw in my mind.

A guy in our unit had a stroke and died just as he left the mess hall. He was only forty-eight years old. Why did that always happen to nice guys?

February Sharon and Chuck moved to South Lyon, a small town north of Ann Arbor.

I officially started work at Quartermasters. Connie brought in sub sandwiches and potato salad for everyone. I enjoyed my new job. It felt great that my muscles complained at the end of the day. I didn't like getting up so early, however, and I'd lost some respect for Connie. While she was a hard worker, she'd been married and divorced three times and I suspected she was involved with someone here.

April Connie got caught. She and her inmate clerk were discovered. I was questioned, but didn't know much (I'd just wondered).

Then I was questioned again about Connie, who had been banned from Lakeland. Half a dozen guards came in to search and our counselor questioned Wally and me a third time. We said we had nothing to do with what Connie did. Then I was questioned again by an inspector:

Inspector: "If you'd caught Connie and Gene 'doing it'

167

would you tell me?"

Me: "No."

Inspector: "Why?"

Me: "Because it would have nothing to do with me and I'd consider it none of my business."

Inspector: "If I told you it was strictly 'off the record' would you tell me?"

Me: "No"

Inspector: "Why not?"

Me: "Because I'd never have any trust in it staying off the record."

He concluded I was honest. I felt sorry that Connie lost her job over an inmate, especially one who only loved himself.

Kris was dating Lynn whom he'd met online and they seemed like a good match.

I started an ink drawing of an old hollow stump surrounded by rocks.

Flores left as my roommate, but not because the board changed its mind to let him go home. Instead, he was diagnosed with sleep apnea and left Lakeland to go to DWHC for surgery. After he left, I had a series of roommates who soon got tickets and went back to the dayroom. I asked to move back to the cubes again, and made a new friend, a Christian named Larry. Larry was smart but worried about everything.

May Diane was here again for our anniversary; she was still the best part of my whole life.

Jerry, the warehouse boss, invited Wally and me to have lunch at Food Tech–big western omelets with all the trimmings–because we'd handled Quartermasters so well without a supervisor.

June My friend Larry's pen pal Susan came to meet him. She was a young Christian woman who lived and worked for

168

a mission in Nairobi. He fretted that Susan wouldn't like him in person, but she did. They continued to write once she went back to Kenya.

July I finally got help to unload the heavy supplies our trucks delivered. Lifting them alone had made my back ache. One of my fingers ached too; it locked itself down whenever I bent it, then hurt like the dickens when I pulled it up again. I was feeling my age.

Kris wrote me that he and Lynn were engaged. Diane and Chandra had met and liked Lynn. They planned their wedding for the end of August in her Massachusetts hometown, so Lynn could get back to teaching her third graders in Poughkeepsie in the fall.

Sharon, Chuck and his mother Esther came for a visit. I really enjoyed seeing them, especially Esther.

August Diane was here in Michigan, and again, I missed her as soon as she'd left. Our visits were always both serious and fun. In warm weather, we could sit outside at picnic tables to visit.

I finally got called to health services for my finger. It was still very painful and frozen in my palm most of the time. The physician's assistant said I had a trigger finger and he gave me the tests needed for surgery to fix it.

November Health services kept telling me I was being scheduled for finger surgery and I kept waiting.

December Kris and his new wife, Lynn, came to Michigan and visited. I liked her and they seemed quite happy.

I finally had finger surgery at DWHC. My hand bandaged, I went back to Lakeland and had to work left-handed but managed. I felt blessed; I was busy, enjoyed my job, and had a wonderful family. I wouldn't feel depressed this coming Christmas.

Diane spent Christmas in New York with her kids and friends, so I didn't worry about her driving on the icy Pennsylvania highways. My hand was healing well and only hurt if I overused it.

A Christian brother died of a heart attack and he was only thirty-nine. It was sad because he was going to be paroled the end of next February, and instead, died in prison. Why was I still alive at fifty-seven?

On Christmas Day an inmate tried to escape but was shot down on the fence. Two guys in my unit got into a silly argument about whose turn it was to use the microwave, and one ended up in the hospital. That's the way we celebrated our Lord's birth in prison.

My hand was healing if I didn't stress it and exercised it with a rubber ball. I tried to finish a drawing as a Christmas gift to Diane; but my hand didn't cooperate.

1995

January Our quartermaster area expanded into a section of the recreation hall as more men came into the prison. The rest of the recreation hall would hold bunks for our swelling inmate population. We were down to a three-man work crew and working until seven or eight every evening.

We had "practice pack up" drills nearly every day. Anything that didn't fit in our trunks and a duffle bag was confiscated. Keeping everything put away and working long days made it nearly impossible to do any art work, but I did. The deputy warden came by, saw a few drawings I was doing on my bunk and praised me until I was embarrassed.

February More new rules: all visitors had to present two pieces of identification plus a social security card to come in, even children. As much as I welcomed visits, I hated to put my visitors through more hassles and was ashamed they had to see me a prison. Prison rules changed so often that what I did (or had) might be wrong tomorrow.

Another shakedown in Quartermaster's. Nothing had been missing since I started there, but the inspector insisted someone was stealing property. We had a good crew who didn't steal, worked steadily, and we were discouraged by the accusations. The inspector's suspicions actually were good for

170

us, because he turned over handling all personal property to the control center, and we only had to handle the prison-issued property.

March The deputy warden wanted to remove doors from the honor rooms, making it easy for anyone to steal stuff. A locked door made it harder for anyone but staff to get into our room. We protested, so he backed off.

We heard that four second-degree lifers were granted public hearings, which was a necessary step toward release. These were the first lifer hearings the board had held for several years. The MDOC needed bed space and all the county jails that they'd temporarily used were jammed full too. Were more people convicted because judges were harsher or because Michigan's crime rate was rising? I suspected it was because the MDOC kept inmates in prison longer, which meant over-crowded prisons.

I was glad that these four might be paroled, but wondered why God didn't help me go home. I could not undo my past–what I did or what was done with me–but I was a new man. Every time I thought of going home, I thought of my childhood and my big crime. *Why did I kill the Rodericks? Maybe because those little kids had to live in poverty and filth, it reminded me how Mom and my stepfathers neglected and hurt me.*

April The women's facility next to ours had a lot of complaints about guards abusing them. The state officials wouldn't let the Feds in to investigate, so the officials had to explain why to a judge.

When I wasn't at work, I made cards and had some drawings going too. I preferred to work on something for a long stretch of time, but with work, chow, counts and shakedowns, I was constantly interrupted.

My roommate went next door to return a tape player and found our neighbor lying on his bunk, dead. Most of the guys who had died over the years were younger than I was.

Our wedding anniversary was a week away, but Diane

was too tied up with work deadlines to come to Michigan. I was so tired of missing our special days. She was the finest woman I'd ever known and even if we hadn't married, I'd be proud just to have her as a friend.

May One Sunday I spent all day on art work and didn't even go to meals. I couldn't wait to finish and show Diane the drawing I was doing.

My board review was scheduled for next year and I was past my minimum sentence, so started gathering information to present. I felt more confident than ever because of the lifer hearings. I asked my supervisor and the unit officers to write me work and unit reviews. All wrote that I was an excellent example to others. I was glad to give those reports to our counselor to add to my file.

Diane helped get my prison history up to date with my jobs, education, art and exhibits. Family and friends sent letters to the board to show continuing support for my release.

June We had a rash of tuberculosis cases in a dozen guys here at Lakeland. We lived so close together, it wasn't surprising. The Atlanta CDC came and tested everyone for TB. I'd had the vaccine so my test was negative. The guards union filed a suit against the MDOC because two guards got TB. By the end of the month, eight guards and over twenty inmates tested positive.

July Guys were still going to the Jackson hospital with TB. Dad was not doing well either; he'd lost a lot of weight.

The DOC backed off on its threats to severely limit our personal clothes, our visitors list and make us give up our TVs and radios. New York prisons took away TVs and had the worst prison riot in the USA. Watching TV is all some men had to do, and it helped the staff keep them occupied and quiet.

By the end of the month, the worst of the TB scare was over, so the MDOC transferred inmates in and out again, which meant more work for us, exchanging their uniforms and bedding. We also got a lot of newly-hired guards, which was a pain because they thought they needed to follow every rule in the book. Tempers were short because of the summer heat.

August Three more men were taken out with TB. We could tell because the officers wore face masks. It wasn't over yet after all.

My co-worker Wally went to Foote Hospital, so I did his job as well as mine and learned to sew and repair laundry bags, shirts, pants and pajamas. This was the first time I'd used a sewing machine and I did fairly well. With Wally gone, I never finished everything in a day, and work piled up. Another worker was caught sneaking some new shoes out and was fired, so we were two men short.

I decided maybe I should leave Coldwater and go to another prison. If I transferred anywhere, I preferred Kinross because the living conditions were best there. I'd have to get a health clearance and an assignment reclassification. I asked our resident unit manager, Haynes, to help.

The MDOC wanted to limit phone calls and visits to family members only and also cut down on the volunteers who came in. Whenever outside contact was cut, we were ripe for riots. We had to mail visitor information forms to family to fill out and return. I thought it was an invasion of their privacy and heard it was being challenged in court.

Haynes had not yet put in my transfer reclassification request as he'd promised, so I barged into his office and told him to take care of it right away. While I was working two jobs all week, he chatted with his buddies instead of doing his job and I was angry. I told him I'd been at Lakeland for six years and nothing had been added to my file. I knew I had work reports, unit reports and security classification sheets made out but where were they? I was the only one at Quartermasters who hadn't been busted for stealing or smuggling dope, yet I had no work reports. At that, he got out my file.

At the end of the day, Haynes called me into his office and had my file out on his desk. I sat there while he went through it and heard him read,

> "Excellent" "Good worker" "Self-
> motivated" "Needs little or no supervision"
> "Trustworthy" "Recommend early release"
> "Stable, has good rapport with staff and
> inmates."

He closed my file and said, "Good Lord, Otto, do you have people on the outside working for your release?"

I said, "Not really. These comments are just from employees here."

Haynes promised to speak to the parole board member who interviewed me next. He finished up the forms and added nice comments about me in his report. I felt much better but was still bitter that I had to push him to do his job.

I was still the only one working at Quartermaster so told the boss I couldn't handle everything myself, no matter how hard I tried. No one else has been hired yet because the suspended workers just finished their hearings, were all found guilty and the boss started interviewing. I said I'd stay and do what I could.

September An officer stopped me in the yard when no one else was around to tell me I should get out of Quartermaster as soon as I could, that "things are going to happen there soon."

Diane wrote that Kris and Lynn were having a baby, our first grandchild. I felt like a "family man."

I quit Quartermaster's. The boss tried to keep me on, and wrote me a good work report. He told me he'd miss me and called me his "best man ever."

October Diane was here. I told her that my transfer request for Kinross was denied because my record was too clean. The officers started calling me "Mr. Too Good." I didn't know what I'd do next so talked it over with Diane. I could go back to work, but $1.46 a day wasn't worth it.

Larry and I teamed up to make Christmas stationery. I

drew the borders, he made copies on the school copier, where he worked as a tutor. Then I added color to the black-and-white copies.

November I called Diane; she told me that Dad was back in the hospital and his heart was failing. She also said Lynn was having a girl and she would see her tiny granddaughter during Lynn's next ultrasound.

Becoming a grandfather reminded me that I was fifty eight and had missed so much in life. I thought of my friends who were younger than me and who had died. Each time I heard of another death, I wondered "Will I die in prison too?" If I knew I had to stay in prison for the rest of my life, I wouldn't mind dying young. But as long as I had hope to go home to Diane, I would try my best to stay as healthy as I could.

December Diane wrote that Dad had passed away and she, the kids and Lynn were coming to Michigan for his funeral. In a way, I was envious of Dad—in heaven, he was truly alive and fishing in the River of Life.

The University of Michigan asked for inmates' artwork for a special exhibit. Diane offered to ship some of the art I'd given her for the exhibit. Christmas was easier this year to get through because I had the art exhibit to concentrate on. I asked Diane to ship my large *Man Without God #202* painting. I also planned to enter my drawing of *St. Peter* and two more pieces I was finishing.

St. Peter   *Man without God #202*

175

The deputy warden asked Diane to ship my art to the prison so they could take my photo with it. He said the publicity would be good for my next board hearing. (It would also be good for him to show off Lakeland.)

1996

January I finished the drawing of St. Peter for the university art exhibit. It was hard with cheap pens that randomly threw out big globs of ink. That's all we could order. Our activities director said he'd loan me some decent drawing pens to finish any other work I'd begun.

"Operation Clean Sweep!" began. We had to get rid of everything that could possibly be used as a weapon … even plastic knives from the mess hall (when filed down to a point, men could stab with them).

March Diane was here and gone for the U of M exhibit and said it was nicely done. Professor Buzz Alexander, one of the show sponsors, wrote to tell me that both of the pieces I had for sale were sold. He sent me a copy of the visitors' reviews and said he'd store the other two pieces of art until Diane got back to Michigan to pick them up.

I still had my original set of dentures and finally was on the list for new ones. My plate was nearly broken.

God's Precious Gift

Evelyn Marie Grainger
April 25, 1996
9 lbs. 2 oz.
21 inches

April I became a grandfather when Evelyn Marie arrived. Lynn and Kris asked me to make her announcement. Diane sent me baby photos; Evelyn was beautiful.

Two new guards were beat up, other inmates got caught planning an escape, five were busted with dope and homemade knives. We also had a big fight in the yard. It was much too crowded and I wanted out, one way or another.

May I called Diane to wish her a happy birthday. Kris had completed his master's degree in business and Diane, Lynn and the baby went to the college commencement. I wished I hadn't missed all the important family days. I was getting older, still in prison, my body was wearing out and I had little hope that the board would parole me. Yet, I would not give up!

June I wrote a cover letter to the parole board to send with my activities report. I admitted that before I met Jesus, I was a hateful, rotten person. I hoped they would see the change in me. Diane wrote to reassure me that even if the board turned me down, she would stick with me. I had the best wife in the world.

Kris and Lynn came to see me, but the baby wasn't allowed in. We sat outside at a picnic table under an umbrella.

July I talked to the school principal here; they'd have some openings in self-study computer classes in the fall. I passed the school's tests, so was ready to start at the next opening. It would give me something productive and interesting to do with my time.

August I was scheduled to see the parole board in two months. I had twenty-five years in now and some of the officers said they'd vouch for me.

September A group of law students at the U of M law school were taking on some cases of inmates fifty-five and older. Maybe they'd take on mine?–but they didn't.

I started the computer class. We were on our own but had a tutor to help in case we got stuck.

Larry's Nairobi pen pal, Susan, was coming again, flying into New York. From there, she and Diane planned to drive to Coldwater together. Larry and I could hardly wait to see them. I was glad Diane had someone traveling with her. Diane's new puppy, Harley, was coming with them too.

October I had my hearing with a woman on the parole board and it was fairly positive. She was very impressed with my information packet, my accomplishments and the fact I'd never had a ticket. At the end of my review, she said, "I should tell you, Mr. Bryan, that because of the makeup of the board–former police officers and prosecutors–they have little interest in releasing lifers. Please don't get your hopes up." I prayed to hear something by the end of the year.

I enjoyed the computer class but wished Diane was here to help me when I got stuck.

November I got a 'letter' from our fantastically smart granddaughter, Evie, with her photo.

December I wished I could just skip to January and get the lonely Christmas holiday over. Diane won't be driving here this year and I had no word from the parole board yet.

1997

January Christmas was pretty nice for me; Larry and I shared some goodies. Diane ordered me the two art books I wanted and sent Larry some money and a drawing book.

February The parole board gave me another flop. I wasn't surprised but hated to tell the family again.

I kept busy with artwork and my computer class. It was hard to do artwork, because every time I'd leave my cube for any reason (meals, shower or class) or when we had an inspection or went outside, I had to put everything away. No exceptions–if I got a ticket, back to the dayroom. We couldn't keep empty containers either, so I had to walk to the other end of our building just to get a cup with water for cleaning paint brushes.

March Larry and I talked about transferring to Kinross. Every week Coldwater got more crowded, and visiting was sharply limited.

One of the officers I hadn't seen in a while–who was an art major–called me into his office one evening to chat. He was angry that I wasn't paroled. He slipped me a really nice drawing pen.

Diane suggested I write my story as a book but I didn't want to. I wasn't anyone special; didn't choose to follow God, He chose me. My art, however, maybe that was a story I wanted to tell, to convey the feeling of how much we all need God in our lives.

April We got a new mess hall, nicer, quieter, cleaner and three times bigger than the old one. It still took as long to get a meal.

I talked with Diane about selling prints of my art online; but she didn't want to do the printing, shipping and handling payments. She still didn't understand how tough it was for me to accomplish anything here. This was really the only thing we disagreed on. I remembered reading in Corinthians that love does not seek its own, so I wouldn't push her to do something she told me she did not want to do.

June I saw the nurse for a checkup. She asked how old I was and when I said sixty, she said I was in good shape. That comment made her my favorite nurse.

I still enjoyed my computer class. I played with the graphics program every time I finished a lesson early. I drew pictures that almost looked like my pen-and-ink drawings.

Some of my artwork done as I played with the computer's drawing program

July My family was moving. Mom had sold their retirement house and moved into a condo in South Lyon, to be near Sharon and Chuck. Chuck retired from teaching and he and Sharon wanted to move south. Diane was considering retirement and if she took an IBM buyout, she might move back to Michigan so Mom wouldn't be alone in South Lyon.

August Because Michigan closed most of the state

hospitals for the mentally ill, those who had committed crimes were sent to the prisons. Had I been committed to a mental institution, as Dr. Tanay wanted instead of prison, I'd be in prison anyway.

September I finally got my new dental plate, and didn't waste any time asking the counselor to put in my request to transfer back to Kinross.

Kinchloe (Kinross)

October, 1997

As I packed at Coldwater, a lot of guards came by, wished me well and said they'd miss me. Soon I was on my way back to Kinross.

I loved the outdoor space we had up north; the sky and clouds were fabulous and reminded me of the clouds I saw as a kid, coming in from the ocean on the west coast.

I bunked in the noisy gym at first. Stealing was rampant, so I kept everything locked up when I left my bunk. My friend Gucci wanted me to move into his room as soon as there was an opening, but first I had to move to the dayroom. If he liked you, Gucci would do anything you asked and get you anything you needed.

November Diane came to visit for a few days; she was thinking seriously about retirement and looking at it financially. She'd have to sell our log house and would move to South Lyon, where she could be nearer to help Mom. She could retire the end of next April, after her 25th anniversary with IBM, and she'd get six months' early-retirement bonus pay.

I did a drawing for our Christmas card while sitting on my bunk (no desks in the gym). Guys asked me to make them cards, but I couldn't do much on a bunk. I'd have to order some more card stock too. Once I got into a three-man room, it would be a way to make a little money. I was number six on the moving list for the dayroom.

Barb came to visit but, because we now had a different warden at Kinross, Bruce couldn't visit me until he got the new warden's permission. Barb and Bruce lived closer to Kinross than any of my family did.

On Thanksgiving Day, we had three great meals: breakfast with scrambled eggs and sausage, dinner with turkey and all the fixings and the great vegetable bar. Supper was large, thick hamburgers, fries, macaroni salad and cherry cobbler. I had missed the good meals here.

Three days later, I moved into the dayroom.

One morning as I stepped outside, a dozen guards came straight at me. I stopped, then a guy came busting around the corner and they swarmed on him. Seems his friend had planned to steal someone's typewriter and pass it to him at the door. The guards learned of the plot and were ready for them. They got him and then went after his inside accomplice, who was armed with a padlock in a sock and bopped a guard in the head. That accomplice went right to the hole and probably had more years tacked onto his sentence. Guys also attached locks to a belt to swing as a weapon, and those things could kill someone.

December Drifting, blowing snow arrived, making it hard to get to the chow hall for meals. Inside, the heat was turned up so high that I sweated in just a t-shirt.

Diane and her two sisters gave Mom a surprise eightieth birthday party; all her friends came by to wish her well. Diane was in Michigan again, but I didn't want her to drive the extra three hundred miles to come visit me in the winter weather.

I got a Christmas card and letter from my old SPSM friend, Doc. His family was vacationing in Los Vegas.

The day before Christmas, I moved into a room. My roommates were decent men and I was grateful to be out of the dayroom. I could leave my things out without a worry there.

Moving to a room helped me avoid my usual holiday depression, and I was finally able to catch up on my sleep. On Christmas day we had ribs, baked potato with sour cream, corn, salad, eggnog, cherry cobbler and an orange to go. During evening count, we each got a quart of eggnog, fudge, chips, cookies and hard candy.

1998

January We had to skate the icy walks between buildings. My old tennis shoes were worn flat on the bottoms and I had no boots yet so I walked very carefully.

I made a small purse from a leather kit for our two-year-old granddaughter, Evie, with a panda face I added on the flap. I thought she'd feel grown up with her own purse.

I saw the doctor, who said I had a gallstone that should come out. It didn't bother me, wasn't fatal and I definitely didn't want to go back to Jackson to Dwayne Waters Health Center), so I ignored it.

Guards found a guy in his room a few doors away on his bunk, with six pencils driven into his chest (one directly into his heart) and an x-acto knife on the inside of his thigh where a major artery was. He was still alive but couldn't speak. His roommates claimed they didn't hear a thing, but were sent to segregation on suspicion. He didn't stab himself, and it was hard to believe they knew nothing. Another lifer tried to hang himself. Obviously, too many prisoners don't value life, not even their own.

One of Gucci's roommates transferred out, so I moved into a room with Gucci and Doug. I got a letter from Flo, my Coldwater roommate. He'd gotten his seventh straight twelve-month flop! I didn't understand… it killed me to see the good guys constantly passed by.

Diane kept in touch with Susan, Larry's missionary friend, through e-mail. Racial and religious conditions in Nairobi were not good, especially for Christians. Both of us were worried about Susan, her mom and cousins there and hoped they could move to the USA or to Canada, where another cousin lived.

February It was a little warmer now, a little snow on the ground, so I got out and walked sometimes. I was anxious to get back to work on some sort of art or craft projects. However, I didn't know what hobbycraft materials were allowed at Kinross, so kept a wait-and-see attitude. The DOC didn't want us to have any tools that might be made into weapons. I understood the need for that rule and learned to do a lot of things with my rounded children's scissors, but I didn't understand how good drawing paper, markers, ink pens or paints could hurt.

Diane was frustrated that I was still in prison and wrote that God may not have put us together for our happiness. True, we didn't know his plans for us, but next to knowing Jesus, our marriage was the very best thing in my life. Diane taught me how to listen, really listen, to other people's feelings and ideas. Her life choices had been a lot better than mine, so I paid attention to her.

March Our power went out one night, not only at the prison but also in the surrounding town of Kincheloe. Even the yard lights around the edge of the complex were off and I enjoyed being in total darkness.

A fellow here died in the bathroom, apparently from a heart attack. He was only forty-one years old.

May Diane retired from IBM with a big party. For her twenty-fifth IBM anniversary gift she selected a grandfather clock, something she always wanted. She packed a suitcase, her poodle, Harley, and came to Michigan for our anniversary. She was the best part of my life and had given me the family I always wanted. While she was in South Lyon, she put a deposit on a new condo only a few blocks away from Mom's. I was glad she'd be closer to Mom—and to me.

June I tried job-hunting, without success. Most of the young guys got the jobs, leaving little for us older men to do. Kinross was calmer and safer than the southern prisons, but

184

also boring.

Diane went back to New York and put our log house up for sale. She was getting rid of things she didn't want to move. Her new condo was smaller than the house.

July Little Eric, who messed up my clothes as he wiggled on visits, had graduated from college and was married. Where did all the time go?

August Mom and Diane went to a family wedding in Wisconsin, and drove through the Upper Peninsula to get there. They stopped to visit me on the way there and back.

September I had my yearly checkup. When the doctor examined my lower abdomen, he told me, "Don't lift weights or do anything strenuous. I don't want to worry you, but you may have an abdominal aneurysm. I'm going to set up some tests." He also checked my lungs, said I had asthma and prescribed an inhaler to use when I got out of breath.

I got a little job, cleaning the counselor's office and earned 46¢ a day. He gave me a nice unit report, bless him!

Diane found a buyer for our log house, a couple who loved it. The husband was an artist, his wife was a writer. Diane sold the extra furniture, scheduled a mover, and waited for the sale process to be finished. The realtor said it might take a month or two.

Health services called me and said not to eat or drink after midnight. I was going for an ultrasound to test for an aneurysm. Results would be back in a week or two.

I was called for a job interview at MSI (the prison's Michigan State Industries) where inmates made inmate clothing and officers' uniforms. The pay was good. The officer who interviewed me asked if I had any problem working for a female boss and I said, "Nope! I've got one at home." She chuckled and replied, "We're good at bossing, aren't we?"

October I *did* have an aneurysm and had a medical transfer request waiting for me. I had to think things through. I may be hired at MSI so had to decide: should I go for

185

surgery or stay and work at Kinross? The physician's assistant explained that my aneurysm (four-inch by two-inch) could burst at any time and I could die if it did. I had to go back to Jackson for the surgery. I didn't want to go, but I wanted to live even more– so decided I'd better go.

Jackson (Dwayne Waters Health Center)

October, 1998

I was up at 6:30 a.m., packed and out of my room by 8 a.m., then I sat in the crowded loud TV room until lunch time with other inmates also going to DWHC. After we ate, we sat a few more hours and finally got onto the hot, crowded bus after four in the afternoon. We thought we were ready to head south, but we weren't. Seemed an officer accidentally took all our ID cards home from work with him. So, we got off the bus and went to the visiting room to get new photo IDs made.

We didn't have time for supper before we got back on the bus to leave Kinross. We went to the Chippewa prison half a mile away to pick up two guys there, and waited until the kitchen made us all sack suppers. We finally left Kinchloe at seven thirty in the evening. It had already been a long tiresome day and we still had three hundred miles to go.

On the way south, we stopped at about six other prisons to drop off or pick up men, and finally arrived in Jackson in the early morning hours. My back ached, my stomach too, from all the jolting and being in a cramped shackled position. All I wanted was to get to a bunk and stretch out. That didn't happen.

Instead we all went to health services for a pulse check. With my medical transfer sheet right in front of her, the nurse asked, "What's wrong with you?" I was tired, aching, cranky and wanted to yell, "Look at my medical sheet, lady!" but I didn't.

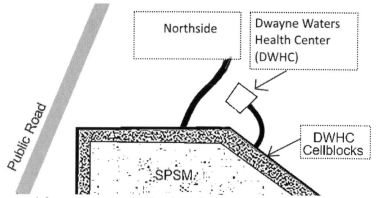

After we were all checked in, we were assigned cells in SPSM. I had to climb the steps to the second tier.

Two days later I still didn't have my property. For several days, I stayed in my cell, in the same clothes, with only a *Rules Guidebook* to read. All I learned from it was that my granddaughter, Evie, could visit me here. After not living in a cell block for fourteen years, I was starting all over again behind bars. Inmates at DWHC for medical treatment were housed in part of the old SPSM cell blocks because some men need to be in maximum security.

I was tired of the coldness, the starkness, the hardness of SPSM. I had nothing to do but stare out of my barred cell, thinking I just wanted to die. It was a little better than solitary in the county jail cell because I had a small window. I could see down the hall, people walking by and a cloud passing overhead once in a while. It reminded me that God was up there, somewhere. My wedding ring was a reminder of Diane and the family, and I realized how blessed I really was. Diane and I shared a closeness that Kay and I never had. I wouldn't give up; I wouldn't be at SPSM forever. My neighbor gave me some paper and a pen, so I started a letter to Diane. She was packing to move and expected to be in Michigan by the end of the month.

I finally got my property (minus a few things not allowed here). Clean underwear was a blessing!

I went to classification again, to DWHC again, to Quartermaster's and finally to the counselor to get my visitor and phone lists transferred. For each trip, I had to call and ask the guard to unlock my cell door. I still didn't have my hobbycraft materials, so couldn't spend time locked up doing any sketching or anything else. Just waiting...

When I saw the DWHC doctor, he felt my aneurysm and said "It's a big one and needs to be taken care of. It's major surgery." I'd been lugging my property around; it could have burst at any time. I got an appointment with a surgeon later in the month.

I wrote Diane that if I died during surgery, to let the DOC or State take care of my body. I didn't want her to pay that expense. My soul was what was important, not my physical body. The DOC did not have custody of my soul; God did!

I finally got the rest of my belongings and was happy to see that the supervisor didn't take out anything. He gave me a new hobbycraft card listing everything as "legal." I spent the afternoon repacking my footlocker. The top tray held all my art and hobbycraft things and the bottom held clothes, papers, my radio, and tape player. I wanted to call Mom to see if Diane was in Michigan yet, but didn't yet have my new phone identification number (PIN). After days of no mail, I finally got it all. Diane, Mom and Barb had written and sent me cards.

I managed to get a minor ticket. When I left for lunch, I put my cell door lock in the wrong hole on the door–so it wasn't really locked tight like I thought it was. (I didn't have to double-check everything at Coldwater or Kinross.)

The food at SPSM was lousy; I wouldn't gain weight, even if I couldn't walk outside. I tried to call Diane. No answer, so I called Barb instead.

My doctor appointment with Dr. Casey was at nine in the morning. I sat in a small crowded waiting room on a hard, steel bench until afternoon waiting to see him. The guys nicknamed him "The Butcher" so I wasn't looking forward to it. When I finally saw him, he warned me that my surgery was dangerous. I said, "Don't worry. I'm too ornery to die!"

He poked, felt my aneurysm and said, "It's a large one. You have a time bomb inside you." He placed my finger where I could feel it. It felt alive, pumping blood. He called Foote Hospital in Jackson to schedule an angiography in a week and my surgery for the day after that.

Dr. Casey told me that after the surgery I'd be as angry as hell at him, probably call him every name I could think of. I told him, "I believe you'll do your best and I have faith in the Lord to take care of me." His secretary smiled at me and said, "I wish we heard more of that."

If my aneurysm ruptured before surgery, I had a seventy percent chance of dying from it. After surgery, I could be impotent or lose some leg function and there was a risk of infection, getting gangrene or losing my leg. I wasn't overly worried, but wished I could see Diane before surgery. She couldn't be in Michigan until the end of the month when my surgery would be over.

While I was waiting, health services called me for a flu shot. They must have been sure I'd get through my surgery or they wouldn't have bothered. I enjoyed the friendly nurses; most of them truly cared about us. I was a medical "00"– meaning I could only leave my cell for a shower, health service calls, and meals. I couldn't go out in the yard in case my artery would bust open at any time.

After my angiography, the doctor told me I had only one functioning kidney, which I didn't know. I went to the hospital, was on a gurney, going to the elevator into surgery when the porter turned and took me back to my hospital room. Dr. Casey came in to tell me that his father was dying in Virginia, and he had to postpone my surgery a few days. I hoped to stay at the hospital, but guards brought me back to DWHC and my cell. I'd had nothing to eat for a day and a half.

Meanwhile, Diane was driving from New York with her dog Harley, the car loaded with everything she'd need for the next month or so. Her furniture was still in storage in New York because her condo wasn't quite finished to move into. She'd stay with Mom meanwhile, and I knew they'd have fun together.

I was "camping" for the weekend and had none of my belongings, which had been put into storage when I left for the hospital. I didn't even have a toothbrush or comb. I did have a brand new unused toilet brush and used it only to comb my hair. I refused to use it on my teeth, however.

November Diane arrived safely in Michigan so I felt better. Without my PIN card, I was unable to call and tell her that my surgery was delayed and that I was going back to Foote Hospital at any time.

Dr. Casey described my surgery: He'd remove my swollen abdominal vein, take a vein out of my leg, and sew it in the place where the aneurysm was. I didn't know where he'd get a replacement vein for my leg, but he must know. Maybe I had more veins than I needed in my leg?

Meanwhile, all Diane knew was that my surgery should have been over, so when she called DWHC and couldn't get any information about me, she and Mom were worried. We learned later that when an inmate left a prison to go to the hospital, no one outside could know in case there was an escape plot planned.

Once my surgery was over, I was back in my cell and when Diane called DWHC, she finally learned that I was fine. An officer handed me lots of get-well cards and letters, smiled and said he'd have to get a grocery cart if that kept up. I was glad to get my latest *Reader's Digest* to read too. I didn't have enough stamps or paper to write and thank everyone. I was tired and very sore, but glad that I came through surgery fine and would heal. I was anxious to see Diane and Mom, but not sure when they'd be allowed to visit.

Two weeks later, they came. I was tired after our visit,

but so glad to see them.

I continued to recover and thought I was healing fine, but overdid it a week later and paid. I'd been taking a short walk each day, stopping to rest several times. I should be able to walk around the track, as well–and I did–but afterwards, I regretted it. I walked to our school, to the shower, to Quartermaster's for a pillow, then to dinner, and DWHC to have my surgical staples removed. I came back and collapsed on my bunk. I still needed to move more slowly and carefully.

December Diane and Mom came to see me every week. My incision was healing nicely but my thigh ached and I still tired easily.

An old friend had a stroke when his brain aneurysm burst, and he was also at DWHC. His whole left side was paralyzed and he couldn't talk. I met two other inmates who also had aneurysm surgery a year earlier and were also still at DWHC. The DOC spent a lot of money on us older inmates, especially with medical problems. That was money they could use for housing younger inmates if the DOC would ever get smart and send some of us home. Were they afraid we'd try to hold up a bank with our canes?

Diane's condo was finished and after the movers delivered her furniture, she unpacked and organized with her friend Menka's help. She invited the whole family for her first Christmas back in Michigan. It was good to have her closer but I felt selfish! I knew she missed the kids and her granddaughter Evie in New York.

1999

January I sure enjoyed seeing Diane every week and kept feeling better. I napped after lunch but also walked outside every day. The only place I was still sore was around my belly button. I hoped to be transferred back to Kinross before long; living in SPSM was the pits.

Diane settled into her condo and found a South Lyon church that she really liked. I was so anxious to sit beside her in the services, worshiping God with her. We had a taste of that during the Prison Fellowship's seminar at SPSM, and I looked forward to that when I was home.

I sent a kite to the Deputy to request a transfer back to Kinross, but a nurse at DWHC said my clearance was only for another Jackson-area prison. There was no medical reason, but I found out I had to see the surgeon before I could be released. He finally gave me a medical clearance, so I went onto the transfer list.

Kinchloe (Kinross)

January, 1999

Going back to Kinross, I was on the bus so missed the Super Bowl. I knew I'd miss Diane's weekly visits, but I was out of that DWHC hellhole. I got a big welcome; guys offered me whatever I needed. I bunked in the Kinross gym again, looking forward to moving into a room. Then I'd be as close to heaven as I could get in prison.

February I felt guilty about Diane having to come so far to see me, even though she agreed it was best for me. She said now that she'd retired, coming to Kinchloe was a vacation for her. I saw the doctor who discovered my aneurysm and thanked him for saving my life. He was surprised that an inmate would be grateful!

Diane sent me good news–Chandra and Rich were expecting a baby in September. They asked me to design the birth announcement.

March I saw the MSI classification director, who put me on the job list. It was hard for older men to get jobs, and I hoped to run the sewing machine. I had a job interview and started work two weeks later. MSI made blue-and-orange uniforms for inmates and grey uniforms for staff at Kinross. My first assignment was to inspect finished work. I left each day, ready to drop, but managed to keep up. I earned 20¢ an hour, $32 a month.

I got a letter from my friend Doc; he and his wife had their own business in Florida.

April I moved into a room and finally got some sleep. I was glad that my new roommates were older, quiet and clean and we got along well. At work, I out-produced even the younger guys. My legs ached, my hips from dashing around and my hands from poking myself with scissors. I moved on from my inspection job, learned to use a buttonhole machine and got a pay raise.

May Diane came for our anniversary and again stayed for several days in a cabin. They allowed her to leave her dog there alone while she visited me. She was glad she'd retired and moved back to Michigan.

The DOC hadn't released any lifers on parole for several years when the Michigan Supreme Court (the state court of last resort) ruled that the "lifer law" (second-degree charges with a life sentence like mine) was a violation of the federal constitution. The ruling could get me back to court, sentenced to a maximum number of years rather than "twenty-to-life" and I could finally go home. When I was sentenced, both the assistant prosecutor and the judge said I was eligible for parole after ten years. The parole board had clamped down on all lifers each time one parolee committed a horrific crime. Laws changed, practices changed until second degree meant "no minimum and no maximum" to the board. A life sentence was just that: you stayed in prison for the rest of your life because of your crime. It was the same sentence as premeditated first-degree murder. The new ruling said a second degree sentence must have a minimum that was no more than two thirds of the maximum. *Life* could not be divided into two thirds.

We had a work break for inventory, so I used the time to work on a possible re-sentencing. I moved into Gucci's room again, and he helped me because he knew just where to find things in our law library. I might be able to plead guilty to a lesser charge.

June Our research found nothing that could hinder my getting a new, shorter sentence. I gathered pertinent law cases and wrote Lawrence to see if he'd handle my motion in court. Looking through my sentencing transcript, I found that it contradicted things: I'd pled guilty to "second degree murder," yet my transcript said I'd be imprisoned for the rest of my natural life. According to the law, a second degree murder charge was *not* for the rest of one's life. I hoped he would take my case.

Barb came to visit and we discussed my anxiety about actually going home. She told me that Bruce was also concerned how he'd do when he first got released.

As I lay in bed, I thought about how much the Bible, Diane and her family had taught me about real love. I had little love in my childhood and didn't realize the difference between sex and love. I didn't truly love Kay, but did respect her maturity and strength.

July Diane came to visit for a few days, and while she drove home, I called to leave messages on her phone that she could hear later.

When I got my June pay slip, I saw a raise to 50¢ an hour, about $80 a month. 60¢ an hour was the most we could earn. (We weren't paid for inventory days or holidays, but did earn extra for working overtime.)

August I moved to a new job on the bar-tac machine, putting a zig-zag weld of stitches at points that might pull apart, such the tops, pockets or edges of sleeves. My day went by faster, I could sit down and wasn't as tired.

Diane came to visit again, this time with Kris, Lynn and their daughter, Evie. Evie was a bubbly little doll.

At the end of the month, Diane's New York friends, Harriette and Paul, came with her. I'd met Harriette years earlier, and was glad to meet Paul. I knew he and I could be good friends. I was touched that they'd come all the way to meet me.

September Surprised, after six months I got another pay raise to 60¢ an hour, $96 a month. That was top pay, unless I opted to be a line foreman or section boss. I didn't want those jobs; too many pressures and headaches. I sent $50 to Diane to get a savings bond for Evie.

Diane left for New York to be there when our second granddaughter arrived. All went well and I looked forward to seeing pictures of Emma.

November I got my first MSI work report, full of high marks about my diligent work ethic and dedication.

Work was hard and tedious but sometimes we had fun. One guy named Joe had worked for fourteen years, was the highest rated in our factory and the bosses counted on him. When one of us had a problem we couldn't resolve, we'd yell "Joe!" for his help. One day we heard a chorus of "Joe!" coming from everywhere all at once. We all stopped work and laughed, even our supervisors.

The guys called me the energizer bunny because I was competitive and hustled to get as many pieces done as I could. One of the guys hung an "Energizer Bunny" sign over my machine, and I got a big kick out of it.

Big news was that all computers would stop when the calendar turned from 1999 to 2000–called it "Y2K" for Year Two Thousand.

December Payday! With overtime, I'd earned extra in November, so sent money to Diane to buy a bond for baby Emma. Christmas was coming and I dreamed of being home with the family. I was grateful to be busy at work so I didn't dwell on it...

A few days before Christmas it snowed and was beautiful, everything decorated in white. Even our high fences and razor wires looked good. Then it got colder, the wind picked up, and we weren't as excited about the snow.

Diane sent Gucci's wife a Christmas card and note, and she was pleased. Even though I wasn't yet home, I thanked our Lord for his birth and life, and that he made Diane and the family part of my life.

2000 (Y2K)

January The new century came and went and the world didn't blow up, nor did the computers stop. We had to go back to work, no matter how bad the weather was, trudging through a foot of thick and heavy snow, blowing so hard we could only see a few feet ahead.

February I had a blood test and my sugar glucose level was high. A nurse warned me to limit sugar.

We worked hard, rushing to produce as many blues (our standard wear) as we could. My shift did mostly shirts; the second shift made both shirts and pants. We worked on difficult items, like officer's grey shirts, raincoats, outer coats, and battle dress uniforms (BDUs) worn for things like riots. Every day I added bar tacks to 450-500 blue shirts, 150-200 grey shirts, 75-100 raincoats, and a few BDU pieces.

The American Friends Service Committee submitted cases to law students to work on, including mine. I added comments about my feelings on the lack of paroles for long-term older inmates. Diane and I had updated my parole board packet, so I included a copy too. I didn't expect to get help from the project, but my input might give the law students some things to research.

March Our work days were cut down to six hours, leaving me more time to answer my letters. It was fifty degrees outside and the only snow left was where it had piled up.

I'd made extra money in February because we had a lot of overtime, so ordered a set of acrylic paints and sent money home to Diane to save.

I didn't have time to start any art projects before new jobs started pouring in. MSI hired more men, and I worked overtime most nights until 8:30 p.m Once our new second shift was trained and ready to work, I hoped to have time to start a painting.

198

Gucci and I sometimes made our own meals, like macaroni salad with last night's chicken breast and veggies from the salad bar. We cooked the macaroni from mac and cheese packages, chopped everything up and chilled it on the windowsill.

We had a young punk in our room and were anxious for him to go home. He was a self-centered goof, and I guessed he'd probably be arrested and do more time again. He was so much like I used to be. He did ask me some good questions about Christianity, sat still and listened (something he rarely did), so maybe there was hope for him.

I got a new work report:

```
Mr. Bryan works in our trim-inspection
area. He does bar-tacking, marking,
trimming, inspecting and most anything that
needs to be done. He is a hard worker that
always works above production. He gets
along well with everyone.
```

May Diane came up to visit again for our twenty-fourth anniversary, my sixty-third birthday. I still felt very content when I was with her.

June We began working overtime again, double shifts and some Saturdays too. I worked even with a terrible cold and two asthma attacks. I had to be rushed to health services and put on a ventilator. The bosses let me leave work and go outside when my breathing got bad, and I had an any-time pass to go to health services. I could even call for our golf cart ambulance if I couldn't walk from one building to another on my own.

July We celebrated the Fourth with an outdoor picnic; two hamburgers or hotdogs, potato salad, watermelon and second servings if food was left over. Once was enough for me.

I had lunch with a guard I'd known at Coldwater who was now also an inmate. He'd gotten drunk, assaulted a police officer and was given four-to-seven years. He was a decent fellow, and Gucci and I hoped to have him in our room when

199

our young roommate left.

I also had an officer friend who, like me, watched the stock market. He'd seen me checking market prices on my TV, and we chatted about investments.

Diane, Chuck and Sharon came to visit me. The Kinross visiting room had two bathrooms for visitors, and Chuck and I sat facing them, while the women sat across from us. We saw a female visitor go into a bathroom, followed a few minutes later by the inmate she was visiting. After this happened a few times, Chuck and I were grinning and Diane and Sharon asked why. We didn't tell them then, but later I told Diane about their dalliance.

After the family left, I missed them so much. I knew that without my family, I'd probably just give up hope about leaving prison.

August I needed glasses but hated the frame selection the prison offered, so found an outside company we could order frames from. I sent Diane my prescription and she ordered them for me.

I had an x-ray because sometimes my hand and arm went numb. It turned out to be related to my job, but I wanted to keep working. Health Services still looked out for me.

November New clothes rules said "No bathrobes" but I kept mine (but didn't wear it). A few weeks later I got rid of it because it took up space in my locker. Then, sure enough, a memo came out saying we could use robes after all.

I turned down a promotion to supervisor at work. The extra 5¢ an hour wasn't worth the responsibility. I'd much rather be a worker and help or fill in wherever I was needed.

Diane and I decided to use some of what I'd earned and some of her savings to get into the stock market. She wanted me to choose the stocks, because I knew more about them than she did. Once we invested, I worried about whether I was right. I sometimes drove my roommates crazy with my "stock talk."

I tackled stocks the same way I'd always done things. I

learned to play a clarinet, practiced and studied hard, then when I got good at it, I quit. With art, I did the same, reading everything I could about a new medium or technique, worked like crazy, succeeded, then moved on to something else. My stock picks were good, then my interest in stock passed too.

I heard that a long-time prison friend died. He'd complained for several years about stomach problems and health services just gave him antacid medicines. He got worse, went to DWHC where they discovered he had advanced colon cancer. He was only in his mid-fifties. I was grateful the prison doctors found and treated my aneurysm when they did.

December We had a couple days off work for Christmas. We'd had snow, but a large parking area behind the housing units was cleared so we could get out and walk. When the sun shone and it wasn't bitter cold, we enjoyed being outdoors. I felt so blessed to have a family and wished I could be with them–or at least hug them–but most of all, I wanted to help make their lives easier.

2001

January My friend Larry from Coldwater finally got to Kinross, and started in the gym. He was still a negative guy, so I knew Gucci and I didn't want him to be the third man in our room. I didn't know how someone with as much Bible knowledge as Larry had could be so negative.

Larry told me that my old friend, Chico, had prostate cancer and was in bad shape. I was sorry to hear that, but Chico was in prison for life, so maybe it was a blessing. Larry told me that part of Coldwater was a medical recovery facility and Northside became a quarantine facility for new inmates. The DOC kept switching prisons around.

Diane told me that our stocks I'd recommended were doing very well, worth more than when we'd bought them.

February One evening I felt good after calling Diane. I took a hot shower, put on a B.B. King blues cassette tape and got out my art materials. Every time someone came to our door to see me, Gucci would tell him to leave me alone and say, "Can't you see he's trying to think and create?" It was true, I was in my own world, thinking of Diane and enjoying my art. I drew a picture of Diane's poodle, Harley, for her.

Diane had houseguests from Kenya. Susan–Larry's friend and also Diane's–told her that conditions for Asian Indian Christians like her family were so dangerous in Nairobi that they decided to leave. They had a cousin in Canada to sponsor them and planned to come to the USA, then request refuge status to Canada.

Susan's two cousins arrived first, stayed with Diane in her condo until Susan and her mother arrived a month later. I was proud about how willingly Diane opened her home to these strangers. Susan and her mother came, stayed at Mom's a few days, then the four of them left for Canada on a Greyhound bus. Mom and Diane loved having them and missed them after they'd gone.

My leg pain got so bad I missed work, in spite of my resolve. I could barely get dressed. Diane had leg and back pain too–we were quite the pair with our pinched spinal nerves. I needed to get approval for an MRI.

March My MRI was denied but a nurse submitted it again. My work supervisor said I could miss work for sixty days, but then I'd be terminated and couldn't be re-hired at MSI for a year. However, she could have me re-classified so I could go back to work as soon as I was medically clear. It paid to be a good worker.

April I saw the PA in health services who told me that I was being scheduled to see a neurologist in Marquette. I think they hoped my pain would go away on its own. However, when the bus arrived to pick me up, instead of going north to Marquette, it turned south out of Kinross. I knew where I was heading–back to DWHC.

Jackson (DWHC, Level 2 & Kinross)

April, 2001

The ride south wasn't as rough this time; only nine guys in our bus and we had comfortable seats. When we picked up our belongings at DWHC, other inmates–who didn't even know me–lifted my stuff and pulled the cart for me.

I finally had an MRI. It was quite a procedure–clanging, banging, humming, dinging and thumping. It showed evidence of some problem so I had a specialist appointment.

I didn't expect the DOC to do anything except put me on exercise and pain pills. Back pain wasn't fatal and I was old. The staff and inmates respected me because of my age and pain, and I got cards and mail from my family and from Kinross friends.

A week later all I'd seen was a physician's assistant who was more interested in the condition of my lungs than my back pain. My whole leg got numb, but the pain was tolerable with pills.

I called Barb and Bruce and got letters from Diane and those cheered me up. The one good thing about being back in Jackson was that Diane could visit regularly.

May I finally saw the neurologist who said I had a herniated disc. Surgery was a last resort, so he prescribed physical therapy. I thanked God that I had a Christian family to encourage me.

Jackson, Level 2

June The DOC was converting part of the old SPSM prison to house Level 2 inmates and I had to pack up again. My poor footlocker was wearing out; I'd moved and banged it around for twenty-six years. I'd have to buy a new one.

We were temporarily housed in "pods," not cells and the place wasn't ready. We had no mess hall, so ate sandwiches, apples and fake orange drink for meals. We were in total lockdown mode, no showers or laundry, and weren't allowed to wash clothes in our small sinks. I was on the top floor so had to climb four flights of steps every time I went for physical therapy. It was so hot that sometimes I could hardly breathe. The guards rarely made rounds so if a man had a stroke or heart attack, he'd die before help came.

Our pods were streamlined and utilitarian. We couldn't personalize them in any way.

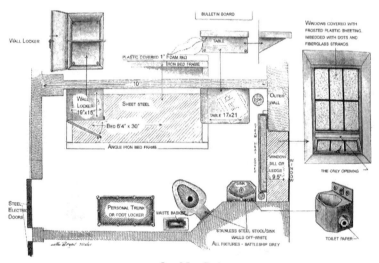

Our New Pods

The old visiting room was under reconstruction, so we had visits in a thrown-together hallway. I was anxious to get back to Kinross. Frenchie wrote that MSI hired two men to do the job I had done.

July Diane and Mom visited me with good news; Chandra and Rich were expecting a second baby.

I saw a doctor who said I'd improved with therapy and could transfer any time, so I submitted a formal request to

Kinross. An officer told me that a bus left for up north on Mondays—so I should be ready. I was glad, but I'd miss my weekly visits with Diane and Mom.

August I was still in Jackson and the officer looked surprised to see me. He brought a counselor to my pod, had her write my number down and told me, "I'll get you out of here, Otto!" It was nice to have a friend like him.

Diane and Mom came to visit often. Mom was frail but still sharp and good-looking at eighty-four. I'd miss them!

The officer checked the list again, but for some reason I was still in Jackson. We were no longer in lockup, however, with some privileges restored. A typical "exciting" day for me went like this:

4:30 a.m.: Bang, bang, bang! Guards let the kitchen workers out.

6:50 I was let out to go to the store to pick up my order of stamps, orange drink and dry milk.

7:45 Breakfast was dry cereal, bread, peanut butter, milk and coffee. Next, out to the yard to walk laps.

9:40 Inside to shower and hand-wash some underwear.

10:30 Laundry bag of blues to base floor for laundry; cleaned and mopped my pod.

11:00 Started a letter to Diane.

Noon Lunch and two hours walking laps outdoors; another shower.

3:30 Downstairs to stand in line for a new inhaler, back to pod.

4:05 Downstairs again to pick up laundry.

4:30 Lie on bunk to wait for chow call.

5:30 Back from dinner; read a new magazine.

5:45 Count time again, sit or lie on bunk.

6:30 Outside to the yard to walk and talk with friends.

7:35 Back to my pods, sponge off and read a neighbor's old newspaper.

8:00 Wash socks, shorts, and t-shirts. Take underwear down from the fan, hang up wet things to dry overnight.

8:45-9:30 Watch TV, then go to bed.

Kinross

September The officer finally took control of my transfer himself. I packed for Kinross. When I arrived, friends came to see me. I'd never had so many handshakes, hugs, and pounding on my back!

The next day, Frenchie and some other guys sent over a welcome basket with peanuts, coffee, creamer and sweetener, and two fudge cakes. I got my new PIN number for making phone calls. I saw a doctor, who promised to get me a TENS unit so I could use its electrical currents for my back pain.

My third day back, I went out to the yard early, listened to some taped Christian music, and thanked the Lord I was back. I received my MSI job assignment.

Then I couldn't believe what happened. Two weeks after I got back to Kinross, I was told to pack up. I got to a phone, called Diane (who wasn't home), then called Barb who said she'd call Diane later and also try to find out why I was transferred. I was soon on the bus heading back to Jackson.

Jackson, Level 2

No one could tell me why I was sent back after only two weeks at Kinross. The nurse didn't know why, and my friends were stunned. I had to move into a filthy pod and worked until nearly midnight scrubbing everything; then I unpacked and fell in bed.

Diane came for a visit and calmed me down. She was the only good thing about being in Jackson again. I waited to see a doctor and sent a kite to the officer who had helped me get to Kinross to ask if he knew anything. I didn't know if he could get me back up north. Before I got any answers, I was called to Classification and asked if I wanted to take a pre-release program. Did the parole board want to prepare me for going home? I hoped so.

October Still no answers about why I was in Jackson. Diane told me that Chandra and Rich were having a boy this time. I hoped they'd want me to make his birth announcement, like I had for Emma and Evie.

I talked to a counselor about my quick transfer to Kinross and back, and he promised to try to find out what happened. Health services ignored my requests for a new inhaler since I'd arrived. Were my medical records lost somewhere?

November I enjoyed the pre-release class and seriously was thinking about what I might do when I was released. I was the only lifer in the class of about thirty-five men. No one knew of any other lifers who had been called for it, and I guessed the class was why I was back in Jackson.

Our housing area was under reconstruction but we didn't know what would happen.

December The unit counselor told me my transfer back to Kinross was in the works and to be ready. I'd just about given up hope. Two weeks later I was still at Jackson and nothing was going on except building reconstruction. The counselor gave me a parole board form to sign, saying it meant they would at least look at my file. Very few lifers had been released, so I wasn't very hopeful.

We were locked down, our pods inspected and all our belongings logged. Then we packed up everything into our trunks and a duffle bag, put them on a truck, and walked from our side of the prison to a partitioned section. We were strip-searched, our belongings inspected and logged, and we got our property back. Guards told us we'd be living in a mix of both Level 4 and Level 2 inmates, and we'd all be treated like Level 4s until the Level 4s were moved out. I'd earned my way out of a Level 4 eighteen years ago!

The end of the month, Sharon and Chuck were back in Michigan for Christmas and came to see me. I'd missed them and still wished they hadn't moved south.

A sad note ended my year; an old friend had terminal cancer; his family was fighting for his release when he died at DWHC.

2002

January The staff was as confused at our move to the mixed section as we were. Health Services called me three times and couldn't find my records. I still had no inhaler. No store orders came in and I was out of stamps and coffee but did have time to start some pen and ink artwork. We had a small high-fenced yard area that was so packed there wasn't much space to walk.

The new place in Jackson was nothing like Kinross. We had block walls in all directions, concrete and steel. The yard was blacktopped, nothing green could grow. Half the phones were broken; the rest jammed with guys trying to make calls.

We had no laundry services except for our sheets and underwear so had to wash everything else in our tiny pod sinks. The warden told us she thought this was the best Level 2 facility in the state—a place with no outdoor space, little to do, five floors high and with stainless steel identical pods to live in—this was "the best"?

I was still classified to work in MSI, but didn't know if I'd be called. No uniforms were made in Jackson, but there was a chair factory, print shop, and textile factory. I didn't expect to have a choice and didn't expect to return to Kinross either.

By the end of the month, we finally got our store orders and security was lessened. I went to work at the MSI chair factory. It wasn't a bad job. I spent the first day stretching and stapling burlap on bulletin boards and learned to put fabric on chair cushions and backs. Stapling canvas was no different than stretching canvas for my paintings so I learned it quickly.

I saw a doctor who said my lung capacity was better—maybe climbing four flights of stairs several times a day helped.

He gave me a colorectal cancer test kit for a fecal smear. I grinned and asked him, "How do I get these back to you, in a kite?"

He laughed and said, "No, just place the name of the nurse you dislike the most on the envelope and drop it in the health services box."

February I was tired after a day of covering chair seats but did find time to do some small ink sketches. I did better than the other new workers, so the boss asked me to show them how to make better seat corners. I also inspected all work at the end of the day. Our supervisor asked me to put together records to account for our tools and stock. It was an easier job and a promotion, but I didn't want to be a clerk. I knew that a couple of my co-workers who worked there longer than I had were pissed that I'd have responsibilities over them. So, I continued working on chairs until my hands were so sore from work that I couldn't draw or write letters for a while.

I did make our new grandson's birth announcement; Albert Richard Burkhart the Fourth was named after his father and grandfathers.

Albert Richard Burkhart IV
Born February 18, 2002
9lbs. 4 oz. 19 1/2" long
Proud parents: Rich & Chandra

Our boss asked me to organize the office tool and supply cage. I painted a sheet of plywood white and outlined shadows of tools in black. He was pleased that he had more space for his office area.

The parole board said someone would see me for an

interview to discuss my responsibility for my past and my future plans. I hated bringing up my past, but did have a positive record for the past twenty-seven years. I started praying and had hope again.

April I was dog-tired at the end of each week, but I did enjoy my work and felt good when I'd finished a big fine-looking office chair and knew that I'd done it. Some of the chairs we built were worth at least $1,000, had expensive fabrics, mechanical options for lumbar support, swiveling, and headrests. Our boss announced that I was his "acting supervisor"—and if anyone on the crew objected, to talk to him about it. I got no pay raise but a couple of men were very unhappy because I'd had less experience than they had.

I was standing in line and felt an inmate fall against me. His body jerked and face got red. He was confused, had trouble talking and couldn't move on one side. Health services came and got him and I didn't expect to see him again. Billy was a good man, fifty-five, had heart problems for several years yet nothing was done for him.

I kept wondering why the parole board was suddenly interested in me. I was the only lifer in the pre-release classes and now the only one called for a hearing. The counselor asked if I wanted someone at my hearing so I asked Diane to come. I also got a letter from a law professor at U of M who was heading a class action suit for paroleable lifers. Was our Lord finally preparing for me to go home?

May Diane visited for our anniversary and we hoped it was the last one we'd spend apart. My supervisor, Bruce, offered to write a work report for the board, even though I'd only worked in the factory four months.

June Diane came early for my hearing, only to find out I wasn't on the parole board's list after all. The same thing happened to several other men, and we never learned why we'd been canceled without notice.

At the end of the month, our counselor gave me another Lifer Review Report form and said I was re-scheduled for the end of July. Another lifer got a new sentence after a court ruled that a second degree sentence of "twenty to life" was illegal. I felt hopeful that it would apply to me too.

July I found out that, again, I was not on the list to see the parole board after all. What was going on?

August Several young inmates got involved in a stabbing on the yard and we heard four guards were hurt during the disturbance. We were locked down again, sizzling in our almost-unbearably hot pods. We had no showers or even running water, because someone might flush drugs or other contraband.

Four days later we were still locked down, had an emergency count, and were herded out to pens in the yard while the State Police searched all our pods with drug-sniffing dogs. The next morning we were still locked down. The factories were closed, so I decided to ask for a medical release to get out of there. Meanwhile, I made greeting cards to earn some trade money. Inmates could pay me with soap, shampoo, lotion and Ramen noodles.

In mid-August, lockup was finally over, and I went back to work. We learned that the chair factory was moving to Ionia, eighty miles northwest of Jackson. Bruce asked a few of us if we were willing to transfer there and train a new crew. The doctor said if my lungs were better, I could get a medical clearance for Ionia, but I'd rather go back to Kinross. I asked Diane what she'd prefer for me; she wrote that Ionia was a two-hour drive for her, and not nearly as far as Kinross. I had to make a decision. Our MSI bosses confirmed we'd continue to work in the same jobs at Ionia for the same pay, and we'd be considered professionals because of our skills. I opted to go to Ionia.

Mom and Diane came to visit for what we thought was the last time in Jackson. We could go to Ionia any day.

September I was still in Jackson, but all the other workers were in Ionia. I was on the list to go, but Ionia was one bed short. My boss said I could keep working on the few chairs that hadn't been shipped yet, so I worked until October to finish up. Then I said goodbye to Jackson, forever.

Ionia (Ionia)

October, 2002

I finally boarded the bus. On the way, we stopped at several other facilities so it took all day to go the eighty miles to Ionia. Our Level 2 pole barn sat on a hill above the Level 4 maximum security compound. We could see the ten by ten cages where Level 4 inmates, one by one, were let out of their solitary cells to get their hour of exercise a day. A lot of the Level 2 inmates had jobs in the Level 4 building, delivering meals to the men's cells, cleaning and gathering sheets and uniforms for the laundry.

Pole barn   *Level 4 building*

It was quiet in the country; farmland was all around us. A local radio station held a call-in contest and the first prize was half a steer. The food was better than Jackson's, and we had an art program once a week, which meant I could order art supplies. I was grateful to be in Ionia.

I went back to work and learned to operate a chair press that eliminated a lot of hard hand-stretching.

November We had our first snow, with little space to get out and walk. I knew Diane wasn't going to drive that far on slippery roads, so we had fewer visits, which was the thing I missed the most. I always felt so content with her and longed to be home more and more.

December I called Diane on Christmas Day, and it lifted my spirits just to hear her voice. The year ended much better than it had started and I thanked the Lord for always taking care of me.

2003

January Our supervisor, Bruce, brought in new inexperienced men to do our complicated work, and we had to re-do most of it. I asked Bruce if I could train the new workers one step at a time, and he said he'd consider my idea. I didn't see Diane much yet; icy expressways kept her from making the drive.

March One morning, three supervisors called me into the office. I jokingly said, "I didn't do it and don't know anything about it." Simon, the MSI boss, smiled and said, "Yes, you did do it and I've got the proof right here!" He handed me an excellent work report and said, "Otto, we know who does most of the work and we appreciate it. That includes our head MSI superintendent. Everyone speaks well of you." I was speechless. Bruce asked if I'd take the inmate supervisor position because he was going to be gone for about two months, and he trusted me to oversee everything. I agreed to do it temporarily.

In the middle of the month, the governor put a freeze on all MSI products because of a complaint that because of our low wages, we were unfair competition for outside businesses. The DOC also had a freeze on expenditures. Those two things left us little we could work on. We could still do work for nonprofit organizations.

I saw the doctor; he listened to my lungs and then we sat and chatted about our families. I was on the prison chronic care list because of my age and medical problems: COPD, intermittent claudication, gallstones, repaired aneurysm, prescription glasses, dentures, hepatitis C, pre-diabetes, a

214

herniated disk, hypertension and osteoarthritis. Old age was creeping up on me.

April Our electrical power went out for nearly three days because of a big storm. No work, no TV, and no hot water for showers. The phones were working, so I called Diane and told her we were camping out.

May We heard we were allowed to make chairs for the DOC again. Apparently they found some extra money, so we would have orders coming in.

Diane came to visit for our anniversary and my birthday. The guys at work surprised me with a silly hand-made card and teased me about my age. They put together a bag of goodies, all my favorite things. Diane also sent me a beautiful birthday card she'd made; I wished I could frame it.

Diane and I worked together to update my information portfolio so I could ask the governor to commute my life sentence. The only bad thing was that a commutation had to also be approved by the parole board before a governor could release an inmate.

Simon showed me a six-foot long church pew with a padded seat and told me we'd get a large order if they liked what we did on this one. He asked me to do it, so I could teach the others. We also had two other large state orders coming. One of those orders was three hundred new chairs for parole officers.

June I was grateful for my job; it kept me busy, too busy to think about my commutation request in process. The board had sent it to the governor's office for consideration. I began training a new young man, Paul, to work in the spray booth. I didn't know then that we'd become good friends.

Sharon was in Michigan and came with Diane for a visit. I really enjoyed sitting between two classy sisters in the visiting room.

In the middle of the month, the governor turned my commutation down. I wasn't surprised, but I hated telling Diane. I felt that I've ruined her life, that she deserved much

215

better than me. I knew her life would be easier if I hadn't told her I loved her years ago.

July We had a great Fourth of July barbeque outdoors with beautiful weather–burgers, hot dogs, potato salad, beans, coleslaw, chips and watermelon. One day off, then back to our busy work days.

This was my summer for classy ladies. Diane brought her friend Menka (who was at our wedding) for a visit.

My hands and arms were hurting, so Bruce asked me to take inventory and do paperwork. He told me he didn't want to send me home as a cripple.

August I hit the jackpot of classy ladies again! Diane and Mom came to see me.

September We had a nice Labor Day weekend; great weather, games, music and a picnic. Regardless of which prison I was in, I always enjoyed the holidays–probably because of the food and a change in routine.

We finally got the huge parole building order; everything new, a $700,000 order for us. We worked on cubicle partitions first, putting fabric on the panels. Then we worked on the new chairs. My hands and arms were numb, so health services took x-rays but didn't find any major problems. I just took more pain pills.

October We all spent a whole day sitting on the hard gym floor for a major shake-down.

I saw a new doctor, who gave me a spacer that helped get more of my COPD medications into my lungs. My blood pressure was running high, so he prescribed more pills.

November Diane, Sharon and Chuck came to see me. I really loved my family and it was hard when they left after a visit. Diane came twice a month when the weather permitted..

December I munched on cashews, my favorite treat, thanks to Diane. She gave me enough money for four bags. We could buy them only during the Christmas holidays.

At the end of the year, a guard told us that the Level 4 prison in Ionia would soon become a Level 5 (the highest security level for the most dangerous men). We'd seen more lights being installed around the yard. We remained a Level 2 and our jobs didn't change.

2004

January For two days, guards tore through the factory, leaving a big mess for us to pick up. They even used drug-sniffing dogs but didn't find anything. When we went back to work, we had to put everything back, then start on a new order for fifty chairs that had to be finished by quitting time the next day.

March I designed a new tool for centering a cushion onto a chair frame base, and it worked quite well. I learned to use the upholstery sewing machine and was glad because it allowed me to sit down for a while.

I got a big plush office chair when a state secretary didn't like the cover material we used for her chair. We made her a new one, then Bruce told me the rejected chair was mine and that I should sit down and use it. He watched out for me.

April I had a busy week–we finished a big order, then had to do inventory. I'd been going to the art class if I wasn't too tired in the evenings. My friend Vargas from Coldwater was also at Ionia and worked for the art instructor. He wasn't released after all, as he'd hoped years earlier.

Vargas had married attorney, Barbara Levine, who headed the CAPPS organization (CAPPS stood for Citizens Alliance on Prisons & Public Spending). They worked to reduce prison costs primarily by encouraging the DOC to release men and women, especially lifers, who could be safely paroled.

Our visiting days changed, and because Diane didn't want to drive home in the dark on weekdays, the only time she could visit was on Sunday, when she'd have to miss church. She decided to come just once a month.

May We celebrated another wedding anniversary–twenty six years. What would I do and where would I be without

217

Diane in my life? I wanted to be home with her, visiting friends and family in Florida and New York. My friend Doc wrote and sent me photos of a trip to Ireland that he and his wife took. Years ago I'd told him that I'd like to go there some day.

I was signed up for a substance abuse class. I'd never used drugs and rarely drank in the past, but my name was on the list for some reason. In class, we discussed how to change our thinking, and the class was interesting. The instructor told us it was important to participate and complete it, because a report went to the parole board.

I was sick again with walking pneumonia, and missed work. Health service ignored my kites.

June I didn't get well on my own, so a nurse finally saw me. I had a fever and my lungs were badly congested. I got some antibiotics and had chest x-rays. The antibiotics helped and eased my coughing so I could go back to work.

I didn't work for long because near the end of the month, the prison tested the back-up generators, we had an emergency count, followed by a shakedown. We started work again, only to close down for another shakedown, this time so guards could hunt for the homemade alcohol called juice that guys were making for the Fourth of July holiday.

July Not much of a holiday; it was a bit crazy with shakedowns, emergency counts, and fights. Stupid jerks got drunk (in spite of the juice shakedown), then acted tough and fought to prove who was the strongest. We faced a long hot summer of more of that.

September We had to scrub and paint the factory for a visit of nonprofit executives who had possible potential work from Steelcase™ and Habitat for Humanity. Once the visit was over, and while we waited for their decisions, we had no work to do, so worked on crossword puzzles and got paid for it.

October My bunkmate was one dumb guy! He threatened to put an officer in a coffin, so was handcuffed and went straight to the hole. Some guys were their own worst enemies.

Two other men in our painting department were fired. They'd made juice and drank it on the job. Sure enough, a supervisor smelled it and they went to the hole. One guy had a parole board review a few days later, but being locked up, had to miss it. It was stupid to throw away a chance for release, just to drink!

I heard that my former bunkmate threatened several more guards while he was in the hole, so he was shipped out to another prison. I didn't miss him.

Guards found juice and a plastic shank that had been made into a weapon at the factory. They also found dice, poker cards and someone's hobbycraft things. We were all locked up while guards searched the whole factory. No work, so I got to sleep in.

November Ionia had changed since I got there. Only Paul and I remained to work in the chair factory, and we were overloaded with orders. We also did some Steelcase recycling work. Our housing unit was full of loud-mouthed guys, and I didn't get much rest.

Finally, our units were split into smoking and non-smoking ones. The doctor said he'd ensure I get into a nonsmoking room because of my COPD and that I'd get a lower bunk because of my back.

December We had another major emergency lockdown just before Christmas; almost ten hours of sitting on the gym floor. Each of us was strip-searched, two at a time. While we sat in the gym, guards tore through our units and belongings, but my stuff was barely touched. On the way out of the gym, we each got a Christmas bag with chips, pretzels and peanuts, a honeybun and a packet of hot chocolate mix.

By the end of the year, I'd been in Michigan prisons for thirty four years, fourteen years past my minimum twenty-year sentence.

2005

February After a night of nonstop vomiting, my face was swollen so badly that a nurse sent me to the Ionia hospital for tests. I had a bad sinus infection; the nurses gave me two injections and put me on an IV. I was so tired that I fell asleep with the tube in my arm. When I got back to the prison, I was on antibiotics and off work for two weeks. It was like a vacation, with meals delivered to my room. I finally felt better, but was weak and my stomach still ached. I went back to work, and the boss told me to take it easy, but we were short two men so I pitched in to help.

I saw the DOC doctor for my regular checkup. Hepatitis was affecting my liver, so he said they'd watch it. The DOC didn't treat men for hepatitis when they were over sixty-five.

March We built four executive desk chairs from scratch for the MDOC director's office in Lansing and finished them in five hours. The people we did the church pews for were very pleased with our work so more pews came in.

I demonstrated how a chair was built to a young saleswoman. The boss told me to choose one I liked, and when I was finished, it was mine! So of course, I picked one of our nicest models and built myself a $650-chair with a headrest, adjustable lumbar and automatic controls that I could sit in at work.

April I still wasn't in a nonsmoking housing unit, so the doctor pushed it for me. Our resident unit manger found me a lower bunk with a window, at the far end of a quiet unit with older fellows. I was delighted and almost glad I had physical problems.

Our six-man units were quite compact.

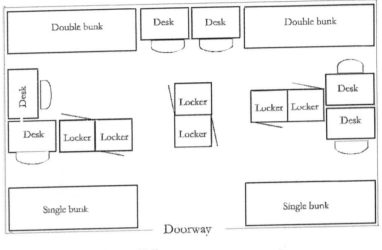

Double bunk | Desk | Desk | Double bunk

Desk

Desk | Locker | Locker

Locker

Locker

Locker | Locker | Desk

Desk

Single bunk | Single bunk

Doorway

Center Hallway

May Diane came for our anniversary. She was facing back surgery in July, and I wished I could be home to take care of her afterwards.

For Memorial Day we had a great outdoor picnic—burgers with toppings, hot dogs, potato salad, baked beans, pop and ice cream. I skipped breakfast so I could fill up.

June My sugar readings and blood pressure were too high, so I had to go to health services for weekly tests.

July We had a nice holiday picnic—breaded fish, potato salad, baked beans, coleslaw, french fries and mixed fruits. The weather was great so we enjoyed being outside most of the day.

Diane had her spinal surgery. Sharon and Chuck came from Tennessee to help her at home. They came to visit me too, but Diane wasn't feeling well enough yet for the long ride.

August Instead of relieving Diane's back pain, her surgery made it far worse, so she went back to the hospital for tests. I tried to call the hospital, but wasn't allowed. I was such a worrywart that I wanted to talk to her myself. The end of the month, Chandra sent me an update. Diane went back to the hospital for a third time to have her surgery re-done by a different surgeon and still had a great deal of pain. She was in a rehab facility to get physical therapy.

September I finally got a letter from Diane. She was still too weak to write herself so dictated it to a friend visiting her in rehab, where she'd have to stay for another month. The guys at work were glad I heard from her because I'd been such a grouchy worrywart.

It was crazy at Ionia; our factory had a shakedown when several guys got caught stealing lunchmeat. They were in top lock for a week. An inmate in Level 5 beat up an officer and another cut himself badly. A fight broke out in my unit, and we had several lockdowns, emergency counts, and shakedowns.

Just when things quieted down, an inmate in Level 5 hit a guard in the head with a cue ball he'd put in a sock. Another guard came to help and there was a big fight; the inmate ended up being stabbed in the eye. Other guards got involved and continued to beat the inmate while waiting for an ambulance. So, another lockdown even for us, and we had to stay on our bunks for a day and night. Tensions were high!

October After the Level 5 inmate was beaten, the State Police and FBI investigated and interviewed inmates, a doctor and the two nurses who witnessed the beating. The involved officers were off work, pending the investigation. The inmates who witnessed the fight were transferred for their own protection. It reminded me of the incident at Coldwater.

December I got word that my good friend Frenchie had a heart attack at Kinross and died. I'd miss him. I also missed Diane. She didn't have her doctor's permission to drive yet so couldn't visit me for Christmas this year. It was the first time we'd missed Christmas together since she'd moved back to Michigan.

2006

January Diane could finally drive, but I told her not to come if there's any ice or snow, even though it had been so long since we'd seen each other.

We were swamped with work again, and everyone wanted their furniture right away. We had a lot of soft line office chairs, couches and sofas to reupholster, fifty to sixty wooden chairs and were getting more church pews to do. Our supervisor hired more men.

My friend Paul became our inmate supervisor, and I trained the new men. I floated around to help with problems when needed and made sure everyone kept busy. The only paperwork I did was to keep the job work sheet information up to date, and Paul did the rest. Simon told the crew I was not to do any stapling, gathering parts or heavy lifting—and they should scold me if I worked too hard. Then our big boss Randy came by to remind the crew that my job was to train, because my experience was most important, and they should not wear me out with manual work.

The "take it easy" business was fine, but it didn't work when we were short of men and facing a deadline. Then, I worked my butt off too. We had a pretty good crew but guys could suddenly be pulled out to work in other areas, be fired or be transferred to another prison.

February A lot of younger fellows were being transferred in. They were loud and smoked in the bathroom, even though our building was a nonsmoking unit.

March We worked steadily all the time; jobs came from state universities, churches, DOC offices, and

223

nonprofits all over the state. I tried to spend all my time training them, but had little time or energy to do any art work in my free hours.

April We had a four-day break because some important MSI supervisors came to check out our factory. While we were idled, I sketched a pen-and-ink piece I called *Institutionalized*. This was almost how I felt; I saw no way out.

May I had trouble breathing and used up my inhalers too fast. The nurse scolded me, said my lungs were a mess and hooked me to a nebulizer, which put a mist of medications into my lungs quickly. She called the doctor, who called an ambulance to take me to the hospital. God was with me there; instead of putting me into a locked inmate room, I was in a regular room with a bathroom and a big TV. I went back to the prison loaded with antibiotics and steroids.

July I had a nice visit with Diane, Chuck and Sharon, then got back to drawing and finished a pair of black cherry ink drawings.

August It is so hot all we could do was sweat. It was too hot to work and even our exercise yard closed.

October We spent six hours on the hard gym bleachers again while our building was torn apart. One of our guys lost a hammer while working on maintenance in the Level 5 building. After sitting in the gym for hours, officers told me they'd found the hammer before we even got into the gym but decided to do a search anyway. What a waste of everyone's time.

I considered a transfer to Thumb Correctional in Lapeer,

even if there was no job for me there. Diane agreed it was time for me to retire too, so I filled out the paperwork for a transfer.

At the end of the month, I was still at Ionia. Diane came to see me and I wasn't very cheerful for our visit. We talked about my earliest big painting, *The Invitation*. I considered it my best painting and had always wanted a good photo of it. The Dankers still had it hanging in their St. Louis home, so Diane offered to pay for a photographer to take a photo for us. She promised to send me a print as soon as it arrived.

November Randy called us all together to say our upholstery department might be moved across the road so we'd have to transfer to the Bellamy Creek facility. I did not want to go, nor did my friend Paul. I'd prefer Lapeer, even if I didn't have a job there. It was half the driving distance for Diane and I'd heard that living conditions were better than most DOC prisons.

December Our boss said he'd put in a good word for me to go to Lapeer. I heard there was a "widget" MSI department at Lapeer where they assembled small parts for outside companies. It would be lighter, easier work that I could do.

2007

January I was still at Ionia, so requested a parole review based on my medical conditions. That could take me home, rather than just to Thumb.

As I filled out the paperwork, I thought back to my first prison experience in Washington. Being in prison wasn't so bad. No one cared about me, and I didn't care about anyone else either so it didn't really matter where I was or who I was with. But after I met Jesus and learned to love others, being in prison and away from friends and family was no longer easy for me.

February Still waiting; I heard there would be a Lapeer ride-out soon, so I was hopeful. The board replied to my

225

request for a medical parole with "no interest at this time."

I got another full-blown nasal infection, so back to the hospital at 3 a.m. As much as I loved to see her, I called Diane to let her know not to visit because I didn't want her to get sick from my infection.

My favorite resident unit manager suggested I write a short letter to the board and remind them that I had nearly thirty-three years served with an exemplary record, was nearly seventy, had serious health issues and those all made me an excellent candidate for parole. I hoped they'd reconsider.

March I woke with my nose as swollen as a balloon and one eye welded shut; my sinuses were full of blood. So, back to the hospital for more tests. The doctor said my blood counts were fine, temperature normal, and I was not contagious, so apparently I'd developed an allergy to the dust or chemicals at work. He said antibiotics, steroid shots plus pills should bring the swelling down. I was off work for a week.

When I went back to work, I did little but even that tired me out. My boss reassured me that I still had my training and problem-solving job, but otherwise should take it easy. I felt guilty when I had to miss work or sat while others were working.

April While at work, things were so quiet I designed a business card for a supervisor's jazz group. I also wrote and re-wrote answers to questions that the board had sent me prior to my next review. One of the school tutors offered to proofread and type my answers before I sent them. Diane came for a visit, and I tried to stay light-hearted and joking so I could protect myself emotionally if things went bad with the board again. I really wanted to go home!

I got a letter from Larry, my young SPSM friend, and he wrote that he was no longer young either. He lived in Oklahoma, had been out of prison for twenty-five years, and was doing fine.

The state police came in to search with drug-sniffing

226

dogs, so we missed another work day.

May My seventieth birthday and our wedding anniversary, and Diane came to see me. We talked about what our life together would be like when I got home. We knew it wouldn't be what we once dreamed of because of our ages.

The guys at the shop made me a card, teasing me about my advanced age. I also got a card and note from my first SPSM visitors and friends, Ruby and Connie.

June Our crew worked hard and fast to finish two-hundred thirty-four chairs, and we finished three days early. I ran from group to group to help, checked the quality, fixed minor problems, and kept everything moving along. We had a good team.

I saw the doctor for a checkup, which included an x-ray, blood tests, talk with a dietician, and eye exam. The doctor wasn't happy that my cholesterol and blood pressure numbers were a bit high. He told me to continue my early morning glucose blood tests plus second tests later in the day. I took a pill for diabetes, but no insulin shots.

The doctor also put me on the special diet line with lots of good, healthy food. I was glad for that!

July My friend Paul's family came to visit him from Texas for a few days. He hadn't seen them in a long time. He was a good worker, and in addition to his own job, did half our supervisor's work for him.

My medical release request hadn't been turned down yet, and the DOC asked for my permission to send my health records to the court, judge, prosecutor, and the governor's clemency council. I hoped that my records would convince the governor that I should be released. In the end, however, it was always the parole board's decision.

A U of M professor and his law students were publicly advocating that the sentence of years-to-life was against the law because the parole board considered a second degree life sentence the same as first degree.

Parole had become very political. Prosecutors, judges

and the governor (who appointed the board) were more concerned with being re-elected and keeping their jobs, rather than doing what they promised to do and lowering prison expenses.

They wanted a prisoner to show remorse, take responsibility and behave–but had no measurement guidelines for these. What was enough remorse and how did you show it? Did I have to cry at my hearings when confronted by my crime against the Rodericks? What could I do to show I was responsible? My prison behavior and good work reports said I was, but somehow these didn't show enough to convince the board to give me a parole. And how much good behavior was needed and how could I show that? My lack of tickets, not fighting and getting along with both guards and inmates were apparently not enough either.

We hoped the U of M professor could legally force the board to consider releasing older men and women like me. I felt ashamed that my faith in God wavered. At times, I felt he must have forgotten me because I was still in prison.

August In the middle of the night, a young man was raped in one of the units. It was an age-old prison problem; housing young kids with prison predators. I had the same problem when I was fifteen and at Woodburn. I learned to fight, to get that first punch in without hesitating. Most young guys hadn't learned that lesson before they got to prison.

September The board voted 'no' again to my release. Diane sent a request for my last board hearing records, so we could see the vote and comments. Most members voted 'No' and commented 'No interest at this time.' That didn't let me know what more I could do to earn a parole.

Paul asked me to draw a dragonfly picture for his lady friend, Rindi. The transparent wings were a new challenge for me but they turned out fine.

Diane and Rindi had become friends and they often planned to visit us on the same day, and had lunch afterwards. Paul and I always joked and wondered if the women talked about us and why they put up with us. Of course, we gave credit to our good looks and charming ways, then started laughing. Seriously, we both wondered how we ended up so lucky to have them in our lives.

October Diane came for a visit and told me she was going to New York to see the kids and grandkids. I wished I was going too, as I mentally did each time she went.

My friend Fuzz, whom I'd known since my early days at SPSM, wrote that he also had applied for release for medical reasons. I hoped he'd make it.

I got a letter from Lois Danker. She was legally blind, but saw well enough to get around in a three-wheeler scooter. Frederick typed her letter for her and did much of the housework. I didn't want to think of them getting older or that I could lose my 'first family.' It was hard enough when Diane's Dad died.

November I heard some good news—a federal judge ruled in the favor of us lifers. His ruling stated that the seriousness

and circumstances of an offense cannot be the sole reason for denying parole. In my case, my brutal crime was the only issue that kept me in prison.

December Diane used the new photo of my *Invitation* painting for our Christmas cards and the cards looked great.

Diane and her sisters rented the condo clubhouse for

Mom's ninetieth birthday and her friends and family came from all over, some from out of the state. Kris, Lynn, and Evie came from New York to help Diane prepare food.

2008

January I got a letter from Pastor Settle, who had introduced me to Jesus in the county jail thirty six years ago. I hadn't heard from him in years. He'd retired as a pastor but was still active in his church. He wrote that the old county jail where I was held in solitude was gone; the area became a parking lot.

I remembered how calm and sincere Pastor Settle was as he answered my questions, even though he knew what I'd done. The fire-and-brimstone preachers that came into jails yelling about repentance and change were the last things an inmate wanted to hear. We knew we were bad! Instead, Pastor Settle's quiet calm broke through my shell.

Our MSI boss, Simon, told me he talked to our deputy warden about my transfer, and she would look at my file. I hoped to get closer to home. Ionia had changed since I first arrived.

Gilkey, an officer whom I knew from Coldwater, told me that the the parole board had two roles: one was the review during a hearing, and the other as a clemency board to look at recommendations from the wardens about those of us with medical concerns. Because this clemency board wouldn't see my information packet, he suggested I give our deputy warden a copy, and she could fax it to Lansing for my file.

February I called the Dankers; Lois was in a care home for physical therapy. Frederick said he'd tell her that the parole board might consider my commutation because of the federal judge's ruling about lifers.

I felt good about a possible parole until my supervisor told me that because of my past record, the warden didn't think I was a good parole candidate and wouldn't recommend it. No matter what I'd done since I came to prison, I could never undo all the wrongs I had done in the past. My hope was that, considering my time served, age, medical problems and institutional record, I would go home some day.

I got a notice that I was dropped from the diet line for no reason. I wasn't likely to get it changed back, even though my blood sugar levels went up.

I got some sad news; Kris and Lynn had split up. It would be hard on Evie, but I wasn't totally surprised by the breakup.

Then I got some good news. Thanks to the federal court ruling, the board was forced to give lifers a hearing. Diane could come for mine in May.

I got another letter from Pastor Settle, thanking me for my drawing of a coal scuttle that Diane sent him. He said he remembered having a scuttle as a child.

Coal Scuttle

April As I left work, I had an asthma attack. A friend grabbed my arm and helped me get to health services to be hooked up to the nebulizer. I saw a doctor two weeks later, and he ordered two nebulizer treatments, and re-checked my lungs after each. He ordered me a new steroid inhaler to use twice a day, prescribed steroid pills for a week, ordered twice a day nebulizer treatments and told me to take a week off work. He also gave me a steroid injection for my hip and spent an hour and a half with me.

My supervisor told me if I'd just show up now and then for work, he'd keep me on the roster because we had to have a job to stay at Ionia. With my board hearing coming up next month, I didn't want to be transferred because I might miss it.

A friend suggested I be evaluated by an outside psychologist before my next parole review; such a report could reassure the board I wouldn't commit any more crimes. Diane set me up with Dr. Miller, a consulting forensic examiner. She sent him my information packet that showed my work reports, art exhibits, certificates, education and accomplishments while in prison.

May I was very much at ease with Dr. Miller, and we talked for three hours. For the first time, I told him about my stepdad Dale's sexual abuse. (I'd never been able to talk about it with anyone, even Diane.) I still felt ashamed of it because Dale always told me how bad I was, that it was my fault he had to punish me when Mom was at work. Telling Dr. Miller about Dale finally allowed me to forgive Dale.

I told Officer Gilkey about my meeting with Dr. Miller and he wished me well. Dr. Miller's report came to these conclusions:

> Mr. Bryan was, most likely, a mentally ill person at the time of committing these crimes but is not presently suffering from mental illness… His overall prognosis for continued psychological stability is quite good. It is my opinion, based on my findings, that Mr. Bryan is no longer a risk to the safety or welfare of the community, and he is predicted to follow all direction and orders of the Parole Board and his Parole Agent with full compliance.

I had my parole interview with Mr. Quinlan from the board. Diane arrived very early as scheduled, but we had to wait until almost noon to talk with him and were the first reviewed while several other men with family members waited. He used a video conference setup rather than talking to us in person and we saw him on a monitor.

Mr. Quinlan was in a hurry and very rude to both of us! He frequently stopped to type at a keyboard and took a phone call during the interview. He interrupted what we were saying and was obviously very anxious to get it over.

We were in the interview room for about fifteen minutes. All he wanted to discuss was what I remembered about my crime, which was still very little. That was thirty-four years ago and I was emotionally ill then. The only positive thing that Mr. Quinlan said was that he was impressed with my prison record. I doubted that he'd recommend me for parole because of his badgering approach to talking with us.

June Since my parole hearing, I tried to stay calm while waiting to hear from the board. Officer Gilkey told me that the other parole board members could see and read Dr. Miller's report, so I hung my hope on that and my institutional record. The other men interviewed the same day had been treated like we had and were also waiting for their results.

We learned that Mr. Quinlan resigned from the board a few days after he held our interviews, staying just long enough to report his opinions.

July I started suddenly shaking as I waited for lunch. A friend took me to health services, where a nurse checked my blood sugar—it was down to 57 because of my new medication. The nurse said not to take the medication again until I saw the doctor.

Gilkey told me that the board was still going through all our parole reports, and so far only two lifers were granted parole. I showed him my ink drawing, *Institutionalized*, and

233

told him it was a self-portrait; a man is in prison for so long he doesn't even see that there is another way to leave other than through that locked prison gate. For me, that gate was the parole board. I didn't think I'd ever be released.

Pastor Settle wrote and told me to hang on to Proverbs 3:5, 6: "Trust in the Lord with all your heart and lean not on your own understanding; in all your ways submit to him, and he will make your paths straight."

August A copy of a letter from U of M law professor Reingold verified the rumor we'd heard: the board still routinely refused to consider any more lifer paroles, even though it was against the judge's ruling. As he'd promised, Gilkey supported my transfer to Lapeer, but Mr. Foy, the transfer officer, denied it. I waited and submitted it again. Meanwhile, I finished a pair of ink drawings to send to Diane.

Pair of kitchen implements

Lois, my mentor and longest friend died and that knocked me down. I was grateful that she was in heaven and not in pain any more, and knew I'd see her again.

Diane suggested again that she and I write our story together. I thought my side would be boring because I didn't do positive things like she'd done. She told me I'd done a lot of remarkable things, that together we had a good story.

September Still nothing from the board. Everyone hoped I'd go home, but if not, I'd try again to transfer to Lapeer where I could get back to doing art work regularly.

We had guys break into our lockers all the time now, and frequent shakedowns while we sat in the gym. I had to watch everyone! Were inmates getting worse or was I too old to tolerate them? All I knew was that I'd enough of the prison life; I was so tired of it all.

We learned that the board was ordered to give the court one hundred thirty cases to see if they followed the judge's rulings. We'd heard that one hundred thirteen of their rulings were "no interest in parole at this time." It was certainly not what the judge–or any of us lifers–had hoped for. Maybe the judge would push harder.

Diane scanned my artwork into her computer and sent me small copies for my records. She also made some notecards for me to send to friends.

October My last transfer request had been denied again, but a guard woke me up early, told me to pack up and get to the control center. At 5:30 a.m. I was on my way out of Ionia and headed to the Thumb Correctional Facility in Lapeer.

Lapeer (Thumb)

October 2008

I was happy to see some longtime friends when I got to Thumb, and to learn that Fuzz's first-degree life sentence was commuted to his forty-six years already served.

I was in a two-man room with a double bunk, and we each had a desk, chair, and large locker. The phones were right outside our door and a bathroom just around the corner, which was great for me, as I had to get up several times a night. It was definitely better than a bunkhouse at Ionia! I had to throw away some of my art materials that weren't allowed here, and I especially missed my drawing pens.

Diane came to visit, and because I had no job, she offered to send me money each month. She insisted she had plenty to live on from her pension and Social Security. It was hard for me to accept Diane's support; a man should support his wife.

Thumb was the cleanest prison I'd ever seen. The young inmates had cleaning jobs so phones, door knobs, stair railings and chairs were washed several times a day. No trash around either. We had to keep our rooms neat all the time. I was in heaven! ...well, not exactly. It was still prison. The food was better, plentiful, and we could choose what we wanted. Everything was spotlessly served, and we were allowed to take a piece of fresh fruit as we left the chow hall.

November I saw the doctor for a lengthy exam, with chest and hip x-rays. There were a few older guys here that used crutches or wheelchairs to get around, so I know I could use

236

those if I needed them in the future.

One of the officers saw my artwork–and promptly got me some drawing pens!

December Shortly before Christmas, the weather and roads were terrible, so I called Diane and Barb and said not to drive here. Barbara was nearby at her daughter's house, so she came anyway, and we had a nice visit.

We had an escape attempt and were locked in our rooms on Christmas Eve–not in a gym here. We simply put our ID cards in our door windows where the guards could count us while we lay on our bunks.

On Christmas day I called Diane and talked to most of my family (Mom, Sharon, Chuck and their two now-grown sons were all at Diane's condo). Diane promised to come after Christmas to visit if the roads were better. Whenever she was with me, I forgot prison for a while.

I did a toadstool drawing for Barb who loved hunting for morels in their woods.

At Thumb, we had a unit of men under twenty-one; they lived separately from the rest of us, but we shared the visiting room. These young men celebrated New Year's Eve by tearing fire extinguishers off the walls, ripping up their mattresses, and smashing their toilets. They were so young, angry and in prison–like me, when I went to Woodburn.

2009

January A fellow lifer at Thumb tried to kill himself by slitting his wrists after his parole was denied. My friend Fuzz– a free man–was interviewed on TV. He said a lot of lifers in Michigan prisons could safely be released. We hoped the DOC listened to him. I wanted to be one of the small percentage of lifers who got out too.

Diane told me that Mom's personality and behavior had

237

changed as her dementia got worse. Mom still lived alone and began to fall, so Diane tried to persuade her to move to assisted living. Mom, however, was fiercely independent, and Diane and her sisters couldn't do much but pray for her.

I still hadn't heard anything about my commutation while the lifer ruling dragged through the courts. The judge hoped the DOC and board would make changes before her final ruling.

One morning I began shaking, was light-headed and dizzy so was sent to the Lapeer hospital where doctors did an MRI, EKG and blood tests. They hooked me up to an IV drip but never told me what was wrong.

February I found out I had walking pneumonia when I could hardly breathe. Aides delivered meals to my room, then I got a new inhaler and some prednisone for my sore chest. These all helped me recover.

Some of the men in hobbycraft made wooden items to sell to raise money for an area children's program and asked me to do some wood burning for them. It had been years since I'd done any, but I was pleased that I hadn't forgotten how.

Mom finally stopped driving and gave her twenty-year-old car to Eric. She still insisted on staying in her own condo.

March I moved upstairs to my friend Dave's room, and three guys picked up and carried my stuff for me. My foot locker was heavy with paper and art supplies. Dave worked in the chaplain's office, and we were both involved in the chaplain's Man to Man program, which taught inmates how to become better men. I also continued the wood burning, and started some new drawings.

It was six weeks until the judge would hear from the DOC about releasing lifers, and I talked to the Lord again about going home. I knew the courts were right to imprison me because I took three lives. I'd paid for it with half of my life and more years than my judge intended. God himself forgave me, but the board and the prosecutor (who became my judge after Campbell retired) would not forgive me.

April Mom and Diane looked at some assisted living apartments, but Mom did not want to move from her condo. I wished I was home to help.

May Eric and his family took Mom to visit Esther in Florida and Mom fell; she may have had a small stroke. She fell again and had a concussion when she got back to her own condo. While she was in the hospital, Diane called the assisted living director, and she and her sister Dot moved Mom's furniture and personal things to one of their apartments. Diane took Mom directly from the hospital to a new assisted living apartment. She was safer, had aides, other residents and staff to look out for her there.

July The courts did not give us lifers good news. I decided to file for another commutation to see if the governor would finally let me go home.

September Assisted living was better for Mom, except she still fell, even after Diane and Dot hired additional aides to be with her day and night. She had another concussion, another hospitalization, and then Mom went directly to the nursing home where Dad spent his last days. Alzheimer's took over her mind and body, and she was worse each time that Diane visited her.

Our Man to Man program was over and our chaplain invited Dave and me to take an International School of Ministry Bible course. I was excited, but concerned whether I could still memorize Scripture. The weekly classes were hard for this seventy-two year old brain of mine! The chaplain asked me to teach an art class, but I couldn't handle both.

November I was pleased that I got 80-90 percent right on my tests. It wasn't easy for me to study the Old Testament word meanings.

Diane gave me sad news; Mom went to heaven a month before her ninety-second birthday. The whole family came to Michigan for her funeral.

December Diane continued to come see me once or twice

a month, whenever the roads were clear. I hated to say goodbye after a visit, and angry at myself for being in prison. I didn't know why Diane stuck with me for all these years but I also knew I was far better off with her in my life.

Someone told me that I'd put my own face in most of my drawings and paintings. It seemed that I had.

2010

January Diane had more sad news; her sister Sharon had cancer and her prognosis was not good. Chaplain Hart said he'd ask his church to pray for her, and I knew Diane's church was praying too.

A friend at Thumb offered to help me to sell prints of my artwork online. Diane put together my art portfolio and helped me write my resume for their website. I hated asking Diane to do things for me because I wasn't home to help her with things in her life. The offer fell through, however.

Diane finally convinced me to start writing my childhood memoirs when we had a break in our Bible class.

February I finished another drawing of St. Peter and sent it to Diane. We discussed printing and selling note cards featuring my artwork

240

St. Peter

again because I was anxious to make some money myself. I still didn't feel right accepting Diane's money instead of working myself, but she didn't want to handle the sales and shipping.

March Diane suggested I add drawings to my childhood memoir. I was surprised I still remembered the details, such as what materials Dean and I had used to build our treehouse.

The chaplain suggested Diane contact an art curator in Detroit who was setting up an art show and who was willing to show and sell some of my work.

June Diane and Barb offered to help me write another commutation request. What would I do without these dear women in my life?

My drawings, *Institutionalized* and new *St. Peter*, both sold in the small Detroit show.

July Diane and her friend Menka drove to St. Louis to get my original *Invitation* painting. Frederick Danker was now in his nineties and wanted us to have it. Diane finally met Frederick and his daughter, Kathy, too.

I finished two more drawings, one of Jesus on the scourging post and the other, the valley of dry bones (Ezekiel 37). I hadn't done any real life figures for a long time. Our Bible classes started again too, and I managed to keep up and pass the tests.

August As I wrote more of my story, I sent the hand-written copies to Diane to edit and type. I wondered what family members and their friends who didn't know me would think of me when they read it. It would be the first time everyone knew about what Dale did.

September Diane sent me copies of my latest drawings but I only had them for a short time. My roommate's Mom and Chaplain Hart were both big fans of my artwork so I gave the copies to them.

Sharon's cancer was worse and more treatment couldn't help, so she and Chuck came back to Michigan and stayed with Diane to be closer to their sons and two grandchildren in Michigan. My heart was broken when Mom passed on, but this was worse–Sharon was my little sister! My family was slipping away, so why was I still alive?

Diane ordered photo books that featured my artwork for family Christmas gifts. I wondered if everyone would be disappointed when they opened their gifts.

October Diane and Chuck visited me with sad news. Sharon was gone. I was the one who should be dead, not her. Diane and Chuck met Chaplain Hart; he came in while we were in the visiting room and prayed with us.

November At a Sunday service, we watched part of the movie, *The Passion of the Christ*, followed by a touching message from our chaplain. Our Bible course was cancelled because someone stole the test answers from the chaplain's desk. I reminded myself that I lived in a den of thieves!

December My blood sugar readings were high, so I started insulin. I made twice daily trips to health services and it cut into my writing and drawing time. I moved to a cell closer to health services, so it was easier for me. My new cellmate had very little and because of Diane's generosity, I'd buy him things he needed with some of the money she sent me.

Diane asked me to design our Christmas card so I surrounded Jesus' face with a thorny wreathe, because He'd been born only to be our sacrifice on the cross.

2011

February Barb's daughter Paulette, who lived near Lapeer, offered to print and sell some notecards featuring my ink artwork online.

March I finished a pair of egg drawings that I had fun with and a honeycomb drawing for the Holsipples (Paul kept beehives in their yard to make honey). I didn't have the energy to write and draw that I once had.

Proverbs 16:24
"Pleasant words are like a honeycomb, sweetness to the soul and health to the bones."

Paulette came to visit and talk about my art notecards. She was as helpful as Barb, and serious about selling my note cards. She said she would print, advertise, handle and mail the orders for me. She was an answer to prayer and I felt really good about this and was grateful for her offer to help.

June Diane came for a visit, but I didn't see her. I don't remember what happened; guys later told me that as I dressed, I acted strangely and didn't make sense. Someone took me to health services, and the visiting desk officer told Diane that I had a non-life-threatening medical condition and couldn't visit. Diane drove home and waited for me to call and tell her what was going on.

However, I never made that call. Instead, I went by ambulance to the Lapeer Medical Center for a stress test and ultrasound. My heart arteries were badly narrowed and blocked the blood to my brain. I was transferred to a Flint hospital for a CAT scan, heart cauterization and blood tests to prepare for open heart surgery. The surgeon took sections of a vein in my leg to replace the blocked arteries in my heart–the second time I'd donated my leg veins for my surgeries. I didn't really know what was going on and remembered little of it later.

For seventeen days I was outside of the prison system, with around-the-clock prison guards who were assigned to my room at the hospital. Everyone treated me very well, even the guards. During that time, Diane had no idea where I was or what had happened. Because of HIPPA laws, the nurses and staff at Lapeer were unable to tell her anything, even though she was my wife. Diane and Barb worked together to call everyone they could reach to get information. Some of the staff dropped small hints that I'd been in a hospital, had surgery, and was OK.

Diane e-mailed the DOC website; and was told to call Gary Remensnyder at DWHC. He told her I'd had triple bypass surgery, would be in Jackson for about two months, and she couldn't visit me yet. I had no paper or stamps and couldn't use a telephone so had no way to contact Diane or anyone until another inmate patient let me use his phone card. After we talked, Diane called Barb, then the social workers, who helped me get what I needed.

While at DWHC I got a notice that I'd have a parole hearing soon. Apparently the social workers at DWHC requested it for me. A few weeks later, I got another notice from the board; they'd reviewed my file, had no interest and said they would review my file again in four years.

September Diane was finally allowed to visit, and we sat on hard cold steel benches in a small sterile visiting room at DWHC, very glad to see each other. A week later I went back to Lapeer to finish my recovery. My heart surgery reminded me how fragile life was. I was still in prison, happy to be back at Lapeer, but would rather be home with Diane.

Diane requested copies of my recent medical records and calculated the approximate costs of my surgery, hospital and rehab stays. With the MDOC guards' wages at the hospital, it cost an estimated $84,000. She sent her calculations with a letter to the Governor's office, hoping I might be paroled for economic reasons (he'd asked the DOC to cut their costs). She got this reply:

STATE OF MICHIGAN
DEPARTMENT OF CORRECTIONS
LANSING

RICK SNYDER
GOVERNOR

DANIEL H. HEYNS
DIRECTOR

August 30, 2011
Dear Mrs. Russell-Bryan:
Thank you for your letter regarding Robert Bryan, #137462. Mr. Bryan is very fortunate to have your support.

During the lifer review process, the Parole Board takes into consideration several factors such as the nature and seriousness of the offense, any prior criminal history, the prisoner's institutional conduct, involvement in recommended programs, the potential for committing further assaultive or property crimes, and the prisoner's personal history and growth.

The Parole Board is required by statue to consider all relevant facts and circumstances regarding each case before them, and issue parole only if the Board has reasonable assurance that the inmate will not become a menace to society or a risk to the public safety. Public protection is always the main component of the Board's deliberations.

The Board was unable to conclude that Mr. Bryan would not be a risk if paroled. The Board's decision will not be changed. Mr. Bryan will be scheduled for a Parole Board file review approximately 3-4 months prior to his Official Date of January 22, 2017.

Further, our records indicate that an Application for Pardon or Commutation was received in our office on June 25, 2010. On September 7, 2010, it was sent to the Governor's office for her consideration. On September 13, 2010, we received a response that the petition was denied. Mr. Bryan may reapply in June of 2012.

A recommendation for a medical parole must come from the Bureau of Health Care.

Again, thank you for your letter.

October Barb's daughter was still interested in my greeting card project, and I found a local attorney who might take on my case. Life was looking up!

Health services asked me to sign a Medicare/Medicaid form called *Choices*. I wasn't sure what it was for, perhaps a way for the DOC to get some money from the federal government. Why didn't they just release us older inmates to save money?

2012

June I'd neglected my journal-writing, did little artwork and moved at a slower pace as I continued to recover. Then, I learned that Barb's daughter Paulette died of a sudden heart attack. She had truly wanted to help me.

I heard that my friend from Ionia, Paul, went to Kinross but I wished he were here instead. Paul could get an MSI job and use our weight-lifting gym (which he liked to do).

I drew the same scene of a drawing that I'd first done in 1976, and saw a big improvement in my drawing skills.

1976   2011

July Diane sent copies of my case to the attorney who had offered to help me last year. He'd come and talked to me a few minutes but I was unable to reach him again. Did he think my case was hopeless? I did not like or trust attorneys (other than Lawrence).

October My memory was getting hazy—I forgot my 4-digit phone call code when I tried to call Diane and didn't want to admit that I had become old and forgetful.

November My friend Paul arrived at Thumb and I talked with him in our yard. We lived in different buildings and I didn't seem him often. While Paul was at Kinross he'd been badly hurt after being caught in the middle of a gang war and was transferred here. He told me about Doug Tjapkes, a man who helped those in prison—for free! Paul said Doug was sharp and knew a lot of the state judges and politicians. Doug had started Humanity for Prisoners (HFP) in Michigan and his organization was supported by donations, not fees.

December I got a new inhaler for my COPD so didn't need my rescue inhaler as much. I began to get more health attention than I did right after my heart surgery. The nurses were great every time I needed them.

I went to DWHC for a breathing test and the results

247

showed that my lungs were badly scarred from whooping cough I had as a child, bouts with pneumonia, my earlier smoking and living for years with smokers in prison. Losing oxygen was like drowning and COPD was the most serious of my long list of medical problems.

Even though my body was wearing out, I stayed in a good frame of mind and hoped for a medical release. It had to be passed by the board, but my medical conditions were worse, so they shouldn't turn me down. The doctor ordered a breathing nebulizer treatment any time I needed it and that, plus my long list of medications and other problems, were costing the DOC a lot of money.

I got some "wheels!" The doctor ordered a brand new wheelchair (which I called my Cadillac) with an assigned pusher, my cellmate Eric. He got paid a little and liked it because we could go to chow earlier than the others. I bought us both some Christmas goodies from the inmate store.

I began corresponding with Doug at HFP using our new prison e-mail system.

Diane asked me to draw our Christmas card again, and as I drew it, I longed to be home for Christmas. Maybe next year, I would be.

2013

January Health services asked me to sign a health records request from the parole board. Diane, most of the nurses and I all hoped the board would finally consider a medical release for me.

March Diane wrote a letter to the board supporting my coming home to live with her. This was their reply:

Dear Diane:

Thank you for your letter regarding Robert Bryan, #137462. Mr. Bryan is very fortunate to have your support.

Our records indicate that Mr. Bryan is currently serving a Life sentence for Murder 2nd Degree. He was eligible for a lifer 5-year file review in 2011. A majority of the Parole Board had no interest in his case at that time. Further, in January of 2013, Parole Board reviewed documentation sent from the Bureau of Health Care regard Mr. Bryan. The Parole Board has determined they have no interest proceeding with this case at this time.

When the Board reviews a life sentence, the members consider many factors, including but not limited to, how many years have been served, the severity of the crime, whether a death resulted, any physical or psychological injury to the victim, whether the crime is a sexual offense or involved sexually assaultive behavior, any prior convictions and the nature of those convictions, the prisoner's current age, physical and mental health, institutional adjustment and involvement in educational, vocational or therapy programs.

The Parole Board is required by statute to consider all relevant facts and circumstances regarding each case before them and issue parole only if the Board has reasonable assurance that the inmate will not become a menace to society or a risk to the public safety. Public protection is always the main component of the Board's deliberations.

Mr. Bryan will be eligible for a lifer 5-year file review on or about his Official

Date of January 22, 2017. Your letter will be placed in Mr. Bryan's central office file so that members of the Board may take it into consideration when reviewing his case in the future.

April Because the board turned me down again, I was really down in the dumps until a woman in Health Services told me she wasn't surprised. She said the board commonly did that, then later called a case up again as if granting a parole was their idea, not ours. She told me not to give up hope.

I was a man who was once unloved, unredeemed and unfeeling; that was the "old Otto." Then I met Jesus, battled with who I was, and became a new man with a new heart. The board refused to judge me on who I'd become, but on who I was many years ago. I needed a miracle!

I asked the nurse who handled medical records if I could get copy of my health records they'd sent to the board. She got them and told me to hide them inside my jacket. The records said I had a terminal condition (COPD) and my life expectancy was approximately two years. The parole board had ignored that.

June I no longer had any energy to write letters or my story and even artwork took too much out of me. One of the last drawings I did in prison was of my rock heads. Mostly I went back and forth to chow or health services; otherwise I slept, watched TV, listened to tapes or talked with friends. Even dressing or using the bathroom tired me. I went to the nurse's station often for nebulizer treatments and they always helped.

Diane still visited once or twice a month and didn't want me to give up all efforts to come home.

August Diane and her son Kris came to see me. After our

250

visit, I thought about God's faithfulness to me. He'd never abandoned me like my mother did, and He gave me a family in Michigan who had never abandoned me. I knew I'd see Mom and Dad in heaven when I finally got there.

I was so tired after Diane and Kris left that I needed to get another breathing treatment right away. A nurse told me I might need a portable oxygen tank. That might be my ticket home on a medical release.

Then, before I knew what was happening, I was on my way back to DWHC. My roommate called Diane to let her know I was going back to Jackson.

Going Home

August 2013

August 21 A nurse at DWHC assigned me to a room with a diagnosis of COPD, oxygen-dependent and I was admitted at 3 p.m.

August 22 I was breathing easily and getting around fine. A doctor ordered chest x-rays and suggested I get physical therapy. I felt pretty good.

During the night, I started coughing, wheezing and was short of breath. In the morning, the doctor ordered more tests and asked me to sign a "do-not-resuscitate" order, which I did. I'd already told Diane I didn't want to prolong my life if I had an illness that I couldn't recover from and my COPD was permanent. I just wanted to go home from here to spend the rest of my days with her.

I remembered Romans 8:38-39, "For I am persuaded, that neither death, nor life, nor angels, nor principalities, nor powers, nor things present, nor things to come, nor height, nor depth, nor any other creature, shall be able to separate us from the love of God, which is in Christ Jesus our Lord."

August 23 Another bad night, and I wondered if I had the energy for a long drawn-out parole process. I could hardly breathe, so pounded on my door to get a nurse for a nebulizer treatment. The treatment helped me go back to sleep.

Diane called DWHC regularly and all that the nurses told her was that I was doing OK.

August 25 A nurse came in and I couldn't remember or mumble my own name or Diane's and didn't really

252

understand what she was asking me. What was going on inside my head? The nurse called for an ambulance, and I left for the hospital in Jackson. Doctors examined me and read my chart, which said "altered mental status, too much potassium in blood, renal failure, and severe respiratory acidosis…" Those words just sounded like Greek to me.

August 26 I had more tests at the hospital and nurses put me on a CPAP machine. Because I'd signed the CHOICES form at Lapeer, I became a hospice patient. No treatment, but still more tests. I knew my name, but couldn't follow directions or stand up. I also had trouble swallowing pills. God's Word reminded me to "fear not," so I was calm. I heard nurses say "Phase 2–final stage" and an ambulance took me back to DWHC.

August 28 A doctor gave me morphine, prednisone, blood pressure medicine and insulin. At that point, I was semi-conscious. That afternoon, a meeting of the medical staff and DOC managers determined that I had end-stage COPD and they were not to resuscitate me.

Diane called again to see how I was doing. She talked to Gary Remensnyder, a DWHC administrator who knew what happened at that meeting. He told her that I'd been out for some tests and was doing "OK." They talked about my future placement within the DOC prisons and he mentioned a prison for ill and handicapped inmates.

He was lying to Diane because he knew that I was *not* "OK" or going anywhere else. He knew I was dying.

I was moved to another room for closer observation.

August 29 All morning someone checked my room often; I was confused, very weak, could hardly sit up. It was really hard to breathe, even with oxygen. Because the meeting had officially made me a do-not-resuscitate patient, I was simply monitored. I didn't hear or feel much of anything. A nurse checked me every fifteen minutes, but I wasn't even aware of it. At 2:15 p.m. I stopped breathing and my heart stopped beating. A nurse called a doctor, who pronounced me dead at

253

2:20 p.m. The nurse called Diane to tell her.

~

Yes, I had died, but I felt wonderful! No pain, no trouble breathing. I looked down at my lifeless body in the DWHC bed and wondered what all the fuss was about. Was this the end of my troubled childhood, years of wandering, prison, finally to have a real family? Had I been faithful enough to my Savior? Had I proved myself productive and useful? Had I loved my family enough?

As I stepped into heaven, I heard Jesus say, "Welcome home, my good and faithful servant. Now, you have that closer walk with me!" I was free! No longer DOC resident #137462. I heard the song that I'd sung over and over in the county jail:

Just a closer walk with Thee,
Grant it, Jesus, is my plea,
Daily walking close to Thee,
Let it be, dear Lord, let it be.

I looked around. There was my friend Michael, with a fishing pole in his hand, grinning at me. I saw the Dankers, the Porters, Mom, Dad and others also in heaven. Is that my little sister, Sharon, that I see over there? People I'd loved, all coming to welcome me.

This was not the home I'd hoped for on earth, but it was so much better! It was *really* heaven, with all my dear friends and family! I knew that Diane and the rest would be coming soon too…

~

"He will wipe every tear from their eyes, and there will be no more death or sorrow or crying or pain. All these things are gone forever." Revelation 21:4

254

Epilog

Robert Otto Bryan was arrested 1972, sentenced in 1974 and died in prison in 2013. Otto had a minimum sentence of twenty years; he was imprisoned for forty-one years when he died, in spite of the person he'd become.

According to the DOC's 1982 parole guidelines, with his history and offense, he should serve at least 29 years. In spite of his excellent record within the DOC and poor health, Otto served eleven more years than that.

Humanity for Prisoners (HFP) is the only organization in the state of Michigan that works one-on-one with inmates in the Michigan prison system without being paid. Its web address is www.humanityforprisoners.org/. Staff members personally respond to each inquiry. HFP founder, Doug Tkpakes, wrote about Otto in his online blog:

~§~

September 2, 2013
Sequel, The Pathetic Parole Board
Robert Otto Bryan: 1937-2013
I penned the entry seen below last March, after the Michigan Parole Board gave my friend Otto a flop. I had sent a letter to the board on behalf of HFP outlining all of his medical issues. In typical fashion, the board looked at the seriousness of the crime 40 years ago, but apparently failed to take a good look at an ailing patient, and a changed man.

I was saddened to hear from Otto's widow this past week that his failing body just couldn't take it any more.

With typical indifference, prisoners learned about his death sooner than his wife.

With typical insensitivity, he had been denied a canister of oxygen for his COPD, according to prisoners, because that was considered not unlike carrying a bomb around.

255

With typical inefficiency, his belongings will not be returned to his wife for about 28 days.

The good news is that Otto can breathe just fine now, and he's without pain.

The bad news is that thousands of God's children are still subjected to this cold-hearted treatment.

(Used with permission)

~ § ~

March 9, 2013

The Pathetic Parole Board

Perhaps the single issue over which I feel strongest disagreement with the Michigan Parole Board is this whole matter of compassionate release...freeing inmates who are seriously ill.

As I write this, I'm having a little private argument with the board in my mind. Here's why.

I've been talking to Otto's wife, who has been so kind and patient. But she's about had enough.

Otto has had triple bypass heart surgery while in prison. He has serious heart problems. Not only that, he has Hepatitis C, he can hardly breathe due to a serious case of COPD, he is diabetic and must be checked and treated several times a day. Besides that, he's 76 years of age. An old, seriously ill inmate, who could better be treated at home.

Now one would think that this man would be a perfect candidate for release from prison. He's a parolable lifer, so that's not a problem. Nope. The Parole Board just gave him a flop.

And if it costs $30,000 to care for an average prisoner, you can bet that the state is paying twice that to take care of this man.

Can the board members really believe that this ailing inmate is some kind of a threat to society? He runs out of breath walking from here to the front door.

Do board members think he has not yet paid his debt to society? He has been in prison nearly 40 years!

Now you have just a glimpse at one reason why our prisons are too full, and why we're paying more for corrections than we are higher education. In my opinion, keeping Otto in prison is a crime.

(Used with permission)

Why I wrote this story...

This is a story I felt we had to tell. I was a technical writer at IBM, but never attempted to write a story until now, in my late seventies. This writing is the most difficult thing I've ever done, yet God has given me the desire, skills and stamina to see it finished.

When I learned of Otto's childhood, his crime, and saw who he was after he met Jesus, it changed my life. I thought I was doing quite well. I had a supportive family, two college degrees, was divorced and dating interesting men, raising two teens, a homeowner with a career and good future ... but inside, I was dead.

On a visit to Otto in 1976, as I poured out my problems to this man who lived in prison and in constant danger, he listened with such empathy that I saw the face of Jesus in his face. How could someone who had such a rough life have compassion on me?

We lived in two very different worlds, yet he was content and I was not. How could this be? That encounter turned my whole life around, the same as it had changed Otto's life. Only God can do that!

~§~

Diane Russell

43864127R00150

Made in the USA
San Bernardino, CA
30 December 2016